YOUR PERSONAL
HOROSCOPE
2012

LIBRA

YOUR PERSONAL
HOROSCOPE
2012

LIBRA

24th September–23rd October

igloo

This edition published by Igloo Books Ltd,
Cottage Farm, Sywell, Northants NN6 0BJ
www.igloo-books.com

Produced for Igloo Books by W. Foulsham & Co. Ltd,
Capital Point, 33 Bath Road, Slough, Berkshire, SL1 3UF, England

ISBN: 9780857349415

This is an abridged version of material
originally published in *Old Moore's Horoscope
and Astral Diary*.

Printed and manufactured in China

CONTENTS

INTRODUCTION

Your Personal Horoscopes have been specifically created to allow you to get the most from astrological patterns and the way they have a bearing on not only your zodiac sign, but nuances within it. Using the diary section of the book you can read about the influences and possibilities of each and every day of the year. It will be possible for you to see when you are likely to be cheerful and happy or those times when your nature is in retreat and you will be more circumspect. The diary will help to give you a feel for the specific 'cycles' of astrology and the way they can subtly change your day-to-day life. For example, when you see the sign ☿, this means that the planet Mercury is retrograde at that time. Retrograde means it appears to be running backwards through the zodiac. Such a happening has a significant effect on communication skills, but this is only one small aspect of how the Personal Horoscope can help you.

With Your Personal Horoscope the story doesn't end with the diary pages. It includes simple ways for you to work out the zodiac sign the Moon occupied at the time of your birth, and what this means for your personality. In addition, if you know the time of day you were born, it is possible to discover your Ascendant, yet another important guide to your personal make-up and potential.

Many readers are interested in relationships and in knowing how well they get on with people of other astrological signs. You might also be interested in the way you appear to very different sorts of individuals. If you are such a person, the section on Venus will be of particular interest. Despite the rapidly changing position of this planet, you can work out your Venus sign, and learn what bearing it will have on your life.

Using Your Personal Horoscope you can travel on one of the most fascinating and rewarding journeys that anyone can take – the journey to a better realisation of self.

THE ESSENCE OF LIBRA

Exploring the Personality of Libra the Scales

(24TH SEPTEMBER – 23RD OCTOBER)

What's in a sign?

At heart you may be the least complicated of all the zodiac sign types, though your ruling element is Air, and that is always going to supply some surprises. Diplomatic, kind and affectionate, your nature blows like a refreshing breeze through the lives of almost anyone you meet. It isn't like you to be gloomy for very long at a time, and you know how to influence the world around you.

It's true that you don't like dirt, or too much disorganisation, and you tend to be very artistic by inclination. You get your own way in life, not by dint of making yourself unpopular in any way but rather with the sort of gentle persuasion to which almost everyone you know falls victim at one time or another. Being considerate of others is more or less second nature to you, though you may not be quite as self-sacrificing as sometimes appears to be the case. You definitely know what you want from life and are not above using a little subterfuge when it comes to getting it.

You are capable and resourceful, but just a little timid on occasions. All the same, when dealing with subject matter that you know and relish, few can better you out there in the practical world. You know how to order your life and can be just as successful in a career sense as you tend to be in your home life. There are times when personal attractions can be something of a stumbling block because you love readily and are very influenced by the kindness and compliments of those around you.

Librans do need to plan ahead, but don't worry about this fact too much because you are also extremely good at thinking on your feet. Getting others to do your bidding is a piece of cake because you are not tardy when it comes to showing your affections. Nevertheless you need to be careful not to allow yourself to fall into unreliable company, or to get involved in schemes that seem too good to be true – some of them are. But for most of the time you present a happy picture to the world and get along just fine, with your ready smile and adaptable personality. You leave almost any situation happier and more contented than it was when you arrived.

Libra resources

When it comes to getting on in life you have as much ammunition in your armoury as most zodiac signs and a great deal more than some. For starters you are adaptable and very resourceful. When you have to take a leap in logic there is nothing preventing you from doing so, and the strong intuition of which your zodiac sign is capable can prove to be very useful at times.

One of your strongest points is the way you manage to make others love you. Although you might consider yourself to be distinctly 'ordinary', that's not the way the world at large perceives you. Most Librans have the ability to etch themselves onto the minds of practically everyone they come across. Why? It's simple. You listen to what people have to say and appear to be deeply interested. On most occasions you are, but even if the tale is a tedious one you give the impression of being rooted to the spot with a determination to hear the story right through. When it comes to responding you are extremely diplomatic and always manage to steer a sensible course between any two or more opposing factions.

Having said that you don't like dirt or untidy places, this is another fact that you can turn to your advantage, because you can always find someone who will help you out. So charming can Libra be that those who do all they can to make you more comfortable regularly end up feeling that you have done them a favour.

It is the sheer magic of the understated Libran that does the trick every time. Even on those rare occasions when you go out with all guns blazing to get what you want from life, you are very unlikely to make enemies on the way. Of course you do have to be careful on occasions, like everyone, but you can certainly push issues further than most. Why? Mainly because people don't realise that you are doing so.

You could easily sell any commodity – though it might be necessary to believe in it yourself first. Since you can always see the good points in anything and tend to be generally optimistic, that should not be too problematical either.

Beneath the surface

In many respects Libra could be the least complicated sign of the zodiac so it might be assumed that 'what you see is what you get'. Life is rarely quite that simple, though you are one of the most straightforward people when it comes to inner struggle. The fact is that most Librans simply don't have a great deal. Between subconscious motivation and in-your-face action there is a seamless process. Librans do need to be loved and this fact can be quite a strong motivation in itself towards any particular course of action. However, even this desire for affection isn't the most powerful factor when considering the sign of the Scales.

What matters most to you is balance, which is probably not at all surprising considering what your zodiac sign actually means. Because of this you would go to tremendous lengths to make sure that your inner resolves create the right external signs and actions to offer the peace that you are looking for most of all.

Like most people born under the Air signs you are not quite as confident as you sometimes appear to be. In the main you are modest and not given to boasting, so you don't attract quite the level of attention of your fellow Air signs, Gemini and Aquarius. All the same you are quite capable of putting on an act when it's necessary to give a good account of yourself in public. You could be quaking inside but you do have the ability to hide this from the world at large.

Librans exhibit such a strong desire to be kind to everyone they meet that they may hide their inner feelings from some people altogether. It's important to remember to be basically honest, even if that means upsetting others a little. This is the most difficult trait for Libra to deal with and may go part of the way to explaining why so many relationship break-ups occur for people born under this zodiac sign. However, as long as you find ways and means to explain your deepest emotional needs, at least to those you love, all should be well.

In most respects you tend to be an open book, particularly to those who take the trouble to look. Your nature is not over-deep, and you are almost certainly not on some secret search to find the 'real you'. Although Libra is sometimes accused of being superficial there are many people in the world who would prefer simplicity to complications and duplicity.

Making the best of yourself

This may be the easiest category by far for the zodiac sign of Libra. The fact is that you rarely do anything else but offer the best version of what you are. Presentation is second nature to Libra, which just loves to be noticed. Despite this you are naturally modest and so not inclined to go over the top in company. You can be relied upon to say and do the right things for most of the time. Even when you consider your actions to be zany and perhaps less acceptable, this is not going to be the impression that the majority of people would get.

In a work sense you need to be involved in some sort of occupation that is clean, allows for a sense of order and ultimately offers the ability to use your head as well as your hands. The fact is that you don't care too much for unsavoury sorts of work and need to be in an environment that suits your basically refined nature. If the circumstances are right you can give a great deal to your work and will go far. Librans also need to be involved with others because they are natural co-operators. For this reason you may not be at your best when working alone or in situations that necessitate all the responsibilities being exclusively yours.

When in the social mainstream you tend to make the best of yourself by simply being what you naturally are. You don't need frills and fancies. Libra is able to make the best sort of impression by using the natural qualities inherent in the sign. As a result, your natural poise, your ability to cut through social divisions, your intelligence and your adaptability should all ensure that you remain popular.

What may occasionally prove difficult is being quite as dominant as the world assumes you ought to be. Many people equate efficiency with power. This is not the way of people born under the Scales, and you need to make that fact plain to anyone who seems to have the desire to shape you.

The impressions you give

Although the adage 'what you see is what you get' may be truer for Libra than for any of its companion signs, it can't be exclusively the case. However, under almost all circumstances you are likely to make friends. You are a much shrewder operator than sometimes appears to be the case and tend to weigh things in the balance very carefully. Libra can be most things to most people, and that's the sort of adaptability that ensures success at both a social and a professional level.

The chances are that you are already well respected and deeply liked by most of the people you know. This isn't so surprising since you are not inclined to make waves of any sort. Whether or not this leads to you achieving the degree of overall success that you deserve in life is quite a different matter. When impressions count you don't tend to let yourself down, or the people who rely on you. Adapting yourself to suit different circumstances is the meat and drink of your basic nature and you have plenty of poise and charm to disarm even the most awkward of people.

In affairs of the heart you are equally adept at putting others at their ease. There is very little difficulty involved in getting people to show their affection for you and when it comes to romance you are one of the most successful practitioners to be found anywhere. The only slight problem in this area of life, as with others, is that you are so talented at offering people what they want that you might not always be living the sort of life that genuinely suits you. Maybe giving the right impression is a little too important for Libra. A deeper form of honesty from the start would prevent you from having to show a less charming side to your nature in the end.

In most circumstances you can be relied upon to exhibit a warm, affectionate, kind, sincere and interesting face to the world at large. As long as this underpins truthfulness it's hard to understand how Libra could really go far wrong.

The way forward

You must already be fairly confident that you have the necessary skills and natural abilities to get on well in a world that is also filled with other people. From infancy most Librans learn how to rub along with others, whilst offering every indication that they are both adaptable and amenable to change. Your chameleon-like ability to 'change colour' in order to suit prevailing circumstances means that you occasionally drop back to being part of the wallpaper in the estimation of at least some people. A greater ability to make an impression probably would not go amiss sometimes, but making a big fuss isn't your way and you actively seek an uncomplicated sort of life.

Balance is everything to Libra, a fact that means there are times when you end up with nothing at all. What needs to be remembered is that there are occasions when everyone simply has to make a decision. This is the hardest thing in the world for you to do but when you manage it you become even more noticed by the world at large.

There's no doubt that people generally hold you in great affection. They know you to be quite capable and love your easy-going attitude to life. You are rarely judgmental and tend to offer almost anyone the benefit of the doubt. Although you are chatty, and inclined to listen avidly to gossip, it isn't your natural way to be unkind, caustic or backbiting. As a result it would seem that you have all the prerequisites to live an extremely happy life. Alas, things are rarely quite that easy.

It is very important for you to demonstrate to yourself, as well as to others, that you are an individual with thoughts and feelings of your own. So often do you defer to the needs of those around you that the real you gets somewhat squashed on the way. There have to be times when you are willing to say 'yes' or 'no' unequivocally, instead of a noncommittal 'I don't really mind' or 'whatever you think best'. At the end of the day you do have opinions and can lead yourself into the path of some severe frustrations if you are unwilling to voice them in the first place.

Try to be particularly honest in deep, emotional attachments. Many Libran relationships come to grief simply because there isn't enough earthy honesty present in the first place. People knowing how you feel won't make them care for you any less. A fully integrated, truthful Libran, with a willingness to participate in the decision making, turns out to be the person who is both successful and happy.

14

LIBRA ON THE CUSP

Astrological profiles are altered for those people born at either the beginning or the end of a zodiac sign, or, more properly, on the cusps of a sign. In the case of Libra this would be on the 24th of September and for two or three days after, and similarly at the end of the sign, probably from the 21st to the 23rd of October.

The Virgo Cusp – September 24th to 26th

Here we find a Libran subject with a greater than average sense of responsibility and probably a better potential for success than is usually the case for Libra when taken alone. The Virgoan tendency to take itself rather too seriously is far less likely when the sign is mixed with Libra and the resultant nature is often deeply inspiring, and yet quite centred. The Virgo-cusp Libran has what it takes to break through the red tape of society, and yet can understand the need for its existence in the first place. You are caring and concerned, quick on the uptake and very ready to listen to any point of view but, at the end of the day, you know when it is going to be necessary to take a personal stance and this you are far more willing to do than would be the case for non-cuspid Librans.

Family members are important to you, but you always allow them their own individuality and won't get in the way of their personal need to spread their own wings, even at times when it's hard to take this positive stance. Practically speaking, you are a good home-maker but you also enjoy travelling and can benefit greatly from seeing the way other cultures think and behave. It is true that you can have the single- mindedness of a Virgoan, but even this aspect is modified by the Libran within you, so that you usually try to see alternative points of view and often succeed in doing so.

At work you really come into your own. Not only are you capable enough to deal with just about any eventuality, you are also willing to be flexible and to make up your mind instantly when it proves necessary to do so. Colleagues and subordinates alike tend to trust you. You may consider self-employment, unlike most Librans who are usually very worried by this prospect. Making your way in life is something you tend to take for granted, even when the going gets tough.

What people most like about you is that, despite your tremendously practical approach to life, you can be very zany and retain a sense of fun that is, at its best, second to none. Few people find you difficult to understand or to get on with in a day-to-day sense.

The Scorpio Cusp – October 21st to 23rd

The main difference between this cusp and the one at the Virgo end of Libra, is that you tend to be more emotionally motivated and of a slightly less practical nature. Routines are easy for you to address, though you can become very restless and tend to find your own emotional responses difficult to deal with. Sometimes even you don't understand what makes you tick, and that can be a problem. Actually you are not as complicated as you may have come to believe. It's simply that you have a unique view of life and one that doesn't always match that of the people around you, but as Libra instinctively wants to conform, this can lead to some personal confusion.

In family matters you are responsible, very caring and deeply committed to others. It's probable that you work in some field that finds you in direct contact with the public at large and many Scorpio-cusp Librans choose welfare, social or hospital work as a first choice. When it comes to love, you are flexible in your choice and the necessary attributes to promote a long-lasting and happy relationship are clearly present in your basic nature. If there are problems, they may come about as a result of your inability to choose properly in the first place, because you are the first to offer anyone the benefit of the doubt.

When it comes to the practicalities of life, Scorpio can prove to be extremely useful. It offers an 'edge' to your nature and, as Scorpio is a Fixed sign, you are less likely to lose ground because of lack of confidence than Libra alone would be. Your future can be bright, but only if you are willing to get involved in something that really interests you in the first place. You certainly do not care for getting your hands dirty and tend to gravitate towards more refined positions.

Creative potential is good and you could be very artistic, though if this extends to fine art, at least some of your pictures will have 'dark' overtones that might shock some people, including yourself. At base you are kind, caring, complicated, yet inspiring.

LIBRA AND ITS ASCENDANTS

The nature of every individual on the planet is composed of the rich variety of zodiac signs and planetary positions that were present at the time of their birth. Your Sun sign, which in your case is Libra, is one of the many factors when it comes to assessing the unique person you are. Probably the most important consideration, other than your Sun sign, is to establish the zodiac sign that was rising over the eastern horizon at the time that you were born. This is your Ascending or Rising sign. Most popular astrology fails to take account of the Ascendant, and yet its importance remains with you from the very moment of your birth, through every day of your life. The Ascendant is evident in the way you approach the world, and so, when meeting a person for the first time, it is this astrological influence that you are most likely to notice first. Our Ascending sign essentially represents what we appear to be, while the Sun sign is what we feel inside ourselves.

The Ascendant also has the potential for modifying our overall nature. For example, if you were born at a time of day when Libra was passing over the eastern horizon (this would be around the time of dawn) then you would be classed as a double Libran. As such, you would typify this zodiac sign, both internally and in your dealings with others. However, if your Ascendant sign turned out to be a Water sign, such as Pisces, there would be a profound alteration of nature, away from the expected qualities of Libra.

One of the reasons why popular astrology often ignores the Ascendant is that it has always been rather difficult to establish. We have found a way to make this possible by devising an easy-to-use table, which you will find on page 157 of this book. Using this, you can establish your Ascendant sign at a glance. You will need to know your rough time of birth, then it is simply a case of following the instructions.

For those readers who have no idea of their time of birth it might be worth allowing a good friend, or perhaps your partner, to read through the section that follows this introduction. Someone who deals with you on a regular basis may easily discover your Ascending sign, even though you could have some difficulty establishing it for yourself. A good understanding of this component of your nature is essential if you want to be aware of that 'other person' who is responsible for the way you make contact with the world at large.

Your Sun sign, Ascendant sign, and the other pointers in this book will, together, allow you a far better understanding of what makes you tick as an individual. Peeling back the different layers of your astrological make-up can be an enlightening experience, and the Ascendant may represent one of the most important layers of all.

Libra with Libra Ascendant

There is no doubt that you carry the very best of all Libran worlds in your nature, though at the same time there is a definite possibility that you often fall between two stools. The literal advice as a result is that you must sometimes make a decision, even though it isn't all that easy for you to do so. Not everyone understands your easy-going side and there are occasions when you could appear to be too flippant for your own good.

The way you approach the world makes you popular, and there is no doubt at all that you are the most diplomatic person to be found anywhere in the length and breadth of the zodiac. It is your job in life to stop people disagreeing and since you can always see every point of view, you make a good impression on the way.

Relationships can sometimes be awkward for you because you can change your mind so easily. But love is never lacking and you can be fairly certain of a generally happy life. Over-indulging is always a potential problem for Air-sign people such as yourself, and there are times in your life when you must get the rest and relaxation which is so important in funding a strong nervous system. Drink plenty of water to flush out a system that can be over-high in natural salts.

Libra with Scorpio Ascendant

There is some tendency for you to be far more deep than the average Libran would appear to be, and for this reason it is crucial that you lighten up from time to time. Every person with a Scorpio quality needs to remember that there is a happy and carefree side to all events, and your Libran quality should allow you to bear this in mind. Sometimes you try to do too many things at the same time. This is fine if you take the casual overview of Libra, but less sensible when you insist on picking the last bone out of every potential, as is much more the case for Scorpio.

When worries come along, as they sometimes will, be able to listen to what your friends have to say and also realise that they are more than willing to work on your behalf, if only because you are so loyal to them. You do have a quality of self-deception, but this should not get in the way too much if you combine the instinctive actions of Libra with the deep intuition of your Scorpio component.

Probably the most important factor of this combination is your ability to succeed in a financial sense. You make a good manager, but not of the authoritarian sort. Jobs in the media or where you are expected to make up your mind quickly would suit you because there is always an underpinning of practical sense that rarely lets you down.

Libra with Sagittarius Ascendant

A very happy combination this, with a great desire for life in all its forms and a need to push forward the bounds of the possible in a way that few other zodiac sign connections would do. You don't like the unpleasant or ugly in life and yet you are capable of dealing with both if you have to. Giving so much to humanity, you still manage to retain a degree of individuality that would surprise many, charm others, and please all.

On the reverse side of the same coin you might find that you are sometimes accused of being fickle, but this is only an expression of your need for change and variety, which is endemic to both these signs. True, you have more of a temper than would be the case for Libra when taken on its own, but such incidents would see you up and down in a flash, and it is almost impossible for you to bear a grudge of any sort. Routines get on your nerves and you are far happier when you can please yourself and get ahead at your own pace, which is quite fast.

As a lover you can make a big impression and most of you will not go short of affection in the early days, before you choose to commit yourself. Once you do, there is always a chance of romantic problems, but these are less likely when you have chosen carefully in the first place.

Libra with Capricorn Ascendant

It is a fact that Libra is the most patient of the Air signs, though like the others it needs to get things done fairly quickly. Capricorn, on the other hand, will work long and hard to achieve its objectives and will not be thwarted in the end. As a result this is a quite powerful sign combination and one that should lead to ultimate success.

Capricorn is often accused of taking itself too seriously and yet it has an ironic and really very funny sense of humour which only its chief confidants recognise. Libra is lighthearted, always willing to have fun and quite anxious to please. When these two basic types come together in their best forms, you might find yourself to be one of the most well- balanced people around. Certainly you know what you want, but you don't have to use a bulldozer in order to get it.

Active and enthusiastic when something really takes your fancy, you might also turn out to be one of the very best lovers of them all. The reason for this is that you have the depth of Capricorn but the lighter and more directly affectionate qualities of the Scales. What you want from life in a personal sense, you eventually tend to get, but you don't care too much if this takes you a while. Few people could deny that you are a faithful friend, a happy sort and a deeply magnetic personality.

Libra with Aquarius Ascendant

Stand by for a truly interesting and very inspiring combination here, but one that is sometimes rather difficult to fathom, even for the sort of people who believe themselves to be very perceptive. The reason for this could be that any situation has to be essentially fixed and constant in order to get a handle on it, and this is certainly not the case for the Aquarian–Libran type. The fact is that both these signs are Air signs, and to a certain extent as unpredictable as the wind itself.

To most people you seem to be original, frank, free and very outspoken. Not everything you do makes sense to others, and if you were alive during the hippy era, it is likely that you went around with flowers in your hair, for you are a free-thinking idealist at heart. With age you mature somewhat, but never too much, because you will always see the strange, the comical and the original in life. This is what keeps you young and is one of the factors that makes you so very attractive to members of the opposite sex. Many people will want to 'adopt' you, and you are at your very best when in company.

Much of your effort is expounded on others and yet, unless you discipline yourself a good deal, personal relationships of the romantic sort can bring certain difficulties. Careful planning is necessary.

Libra with Pisces Ascendant

An Air and Water combination, you are not easy to understand and have depths that show at times, surprising those people who thought they already knew what you were. You will always keep people guessing and are just as likely to hitchhike around Europe as you are to hold down a steady job, both of which you would undertake with the same degree of commitment and success. Usually young at heart, but always carrying the potential for an old head on young shoulders, you are something of a paradox and not at all easy for totally 'straight' types to understand. But you always make an impression and tend to be very attractive to members of the opposite sex.

In matters of health you do have to be a little careful because you dissipate much nervous energy and can sometimes be inclined to push yourself too hard, at least in a mental sense. Frequent periods of rest and meditation will do you the world of good and should improve your level of wisdom, which tends to be fairly high already. Much of your effort in life is expounded on behalf of humanity as a whole, for you care deeply, love totally and always give of your best. Whatever your faults and failings might be, you are one of the most popular people around.

Libra with Aries Ascendant

Libra has the tendency to bring out the best in any zodiac sign, and this is no exception when it comes together with Aries. You may, in fact, be the most comfortable of all Aries types, simply because Libra tempers some of your more assertive qualities and gives you the chance to balance out opposing forces, both inside yourself and in the world outside. You are fun to be with and make the staunchest friend possible. Although you are generally affable, few people would try to put one over on you because they would quickly come to know how far you are willing to go before you let forth a string of invective that would shock those who previously underestimated your basic Aries traits.

Home and family are very dear to you, but you are more tolerant than some Aries types are inclined to be and you have a youthful zest for life that should stay with you no matter what age you manage to achieve. There is always something interesting to do and your mind is a constant stream of possibilities. This makes you very creative and you may also demonstrate a desire to look good at all times. You may not always be quite as confident as you appear to be, but few would guess the fact.

Libra with Taurus Ascendant

A fortunate combination in many ways, this is a double-Venus rulership, since both Taurus and Libra are heavily reliant on the planet of love. You are social, amiable and a natural diplomat, anxious to please and ready to care for just about anyone who shows interest in you. You hate disorder, which means that there is a place for everything and everything in its place. This can throw up the odd paradox however, since being half Libran you cannot always work out where that place ought to be! You deal with life in a humorous way and are quite capable of seeing the absurd in yourself, as well as in others. Your heart is no bigger than that of the quite typical Taurean, but it sits rather closer to the surface and so others recognise it more.

On those occasions when you know you are standing on firm ground you can show great confidence, even if you have to be ready to change some of your opinions at the drop of a hat. When this happens you can be quite at odds with yourself, because Taurus doesn't take very many U-turns, whereas Libra does. Don't expect to know yourself too well, and keep looking for the funny side of things, because it is within humour that you forge the sort of life that suits you best.

Libra with Gemini Ascendant

What a happy-go-lucky soul you are and how popular you tend to be with those around you. Libra is, like Gemini, an Air sign and this means that you are the communicator par excellence, even by Gemini standards. It can sometimes be difficult for you to make up your mind about things because Libra does not exactly aid this process, and especially not when it is allied to Mercurial Gemini. Frequent periods of deep thought are necessary, and meditation would do you a great deal of good. All the same, although you might sometimes be rather unsure of yourself, you are rarely without a certain balance. Clean and tidy surroundings suit you the best, though this is far from easy to achieve because you are invariably dashing off to some place or other, so you really need someone to sort things out in your absence.

The most important fact of all is that you are much loved by your friends, of which there are likely to be very many. Because you are so willing to help them out, in return they are usually there when it matters and they would probably go to almost any length on your behalf. You exhibit a fine sense of justice and will usually back those in trouble. Charities tend to be attractive to you and you do much on behalf of those who live on the fringes of society or people who are truly alone.

Libra with Cancer Ascendant

What an absolutely pleasant and approachable sort of person you are, and how much you have to offer. Like most people associated with the sign of Cancer you give yourself freely to the world, and will always be on hand if anyone is in trouble or needs the special touch you can bring to almost any problem. Behaving in this way is the biggest part of what you are and so people come to rely on you very heavily. Like Libra you can see both sides of any coin and you exhibit the Libran tendency to jump about from one foot to the other when it is necessary to make decisions relating to your own life. This is not usually the case when you are dealing with others however, because the cooler and more detached qualities of Cancer will show through in these circumstances.

It would be fair to say that you do not deal with routines as well as Cancer alone might do and you need a degree of variety in your life, which in your case often comes in the form of travel, which can be distant and of long duration. It isn't unusual for people who have this zodiac combination to end up living abroad, though even this does little to prevent you from getting itchy feet from time to time. In romance you show an original quality that keeps the relationship young and working very well.

Libra with Leo Ascendant

Libra brings slightly more flexibility to the fixed quality of the Leo nature. On the whole you do not represent a picture that is so much different from other versions of the Lion, though you find more time to smile, enjoy changing your mind a great deal more and have a greater number of casual friends. Few would find you proud or haughty and you retain the common touch that can be so important when it comes to getting on in life generally. At work you like to do something that brings variety, and would probably soon tire of doing the same task over and over again. Many of you are teachers, for you have patience, allied to a stubborn core. This can be an indispensable combination on occasions and is part of the reason for the material success that many folk with this combination of signs achieve.

It isn't often that you get down in the dumps, after all there is generally something more important around the next corner, and you love the cut and thrust of everyday life. You always manage to stay young at heart, no matter what your age might be, and you revel in the company of interesting and stimulating types. Maybe you should try harder to concentrate on one thing at once and also strive to retain a serious opinion for more than ten minutes at a time. However, Leo helps to control your flighty tendencies.

Libra with Virgo Ascendant

Libra has the ability to lighten almost any load, and it is particularly good at doing so when it is brought together with the much more repressed sign of Virgo. To the world at large you seem relaxed, happy and able to cope with most of the pressures that life places upon you. Not only do you deal with your own life in a bright and breezy manner but you are usually on hand to help others out of any dilemma that they might make for themselves. With excellent powers of communication, you leave the world at large in no doubt whatsoever concerning both your opinions and your wishes. It is in the talking stakes that you really excel because Virgo brings the silver tongue of Mercury and Libra adds the Air-sign desire to be in constant touch with the world outside your door.

You like to have a good time and can often be found in the company of interesting and stimulating people, who have the ability to bring out the very best in your bright and sparkling personality. Underneath however, there is still much of the worrying Virgoan to be found and this means that you have to learn to relax inside as well as appearing to do so externally. In fact you are much more complex than most people would realise, and definitely would not be suited to a life that allowed you too much time to think about yourself.

THE MOON AND THE PART IT PLAYS IN YOUR LIFE

In astrology the Moon is probably the single most important heavenly body after the Sun. Its unique position, as partner to the Earth on its journey around the solar system, means that the Moon appears to pass through the signs of the zodiac extremely quickly. The zodiac position of the Moon at the time of your birth plays a great part in personal character and is especially significant in the build-up of your emotional nature.

Your Own Moon Sign

Discovering the position of the Moon at the time of your birth has always been notoriously difficult because tracking the complex zodiac positions of the Moon is not easy. This process has been reduced to three simple stages with our Lunar Tables. A breakdown of the Moon's zodiac positions can be found from page 35 onwards, so that once you know what your Moon Sign is, you can see what part this plays in the overall build-up of your personal character.

If you follow the instructions on the next page you will soon be able to work out exactly what zodiac sign the Moon occupied on the day that you were born and you can then go on to compare the reading for this position with those of your Sun sign and your Ascendant. It is partly the comparison between these three important positions that goes towards making you the unique individual you are.

HOW TO DISCOVER YOUR MOON SIGN

This is a three-stage process. You may need a pen and a piece of paper but if you follow the instructions below the process should only take a minute or so.

STAGE 1 First of all you need to know the Moon Age at the time of your birth. If you look at Moon Table 1, on page 33, you will find all the years between 1914 and 2012 down the left side. Find the year of your birth and then trace across to the right to the month of your birth. Where the two intersect you will find a number. This is the date of the New Moon in the month that you were born. You now need to count forward the number of days between the New Moon and your own birthday. For example, if the New Moon in the month of your birth was shown as being the 6th and you were born on the 20th, your Moon Age Day would be 14. If the New Moon in the month of your birth came after your birthday, you need to count forward from the New Moon in the previous month. Whatever the result, jot this number down so that you do not forget it.

STAGE 2 Take a look at Moon Table 2 on page 34. Down the left hand column look for the date of your birth. Now trace across to the month of your birth. Where the two meet you will find a letter. Copy this letter down alongside your Moon Age Day.

STAGE 3 Moon Table 3 on page 34 will supply you with the zodiac sign the Moon occupied on the day of your birth. Look for your Moon Age Day down the left hand column and then for the letter you found in Stage 2. Where the two converge you will find a zodiac sign and this is the sign occupied by the Moon on the day that you were born.

Your Zodiac Moon Sign Explained

You will find a profile of all zodiac Moon Signs on pages 35 to 38, showing in yet another way how astrology helps to make you into the individual that you are. In each daily entry of the Astral Diary you can find the zodiac position of the Moon for every day of the year. This also allows you to discover your lunar birthdays. Since the Moon passes through all the signs of the zodiac in about a month, you can expect something like twelve lunar birthdays each year. At these times you are likely to be emotionally steady and able to make the sort of decisions that have real, lasting value.

MOON TABLE 1

YEAR	AUG	SEP	OCT	YEAR	AUG	SEP	OCT	YEAR	AUG	SEP	OCT
1914	21	19	19	1947	16	14	14	1980	11	10	9
1915	10	9	8	1948	5	3	2	1981	29	28	27
1916	29	27	27	1949	24	23	21	1982	19	17	17
1917	17	15	15	1950	13	12	11	1983	8	7	6
1918	6	4	4	1951	2	1	1/30	1984	26	25	24
1919	25	23	23	1952	20	19	18	1985	16	14	14
1920	14	12	12	1953	9	8	8	1986	5	4	3
1921	3	2	1/30	1954	28	27	26	1987	24	23	22
1922	22	21	20	1955	17	16	15	1988	12	11	10
1923	12	10	10	1956	6	4	4	1989	1/31	29	29
1924	30	28	28	1957	25	23	23	1990	20	19	18
1925	19	18	17	1958	15	13	12	1991	9	8	8
1926	8	7	6	1959	4	3	2/31	1992	28	26	25
1927	27	25	25	1960	22	21	20	1993	17	16	15
1928	16	14	14	1961	11	10	9	1994	7	5	5
1929	5	3	2	1962	30	28	28	1995	26	24	24
1930	24	22	20	1963	19	17	17	1996	14	13	11
1931	13	12	11	1964	7	6	5	1997	3	2	2/31
1932	2/31	30	29	1965	26	25	24	1998	22	20	20
1933	21	19	19	1966	16	14	14	1999	11	10	8
1934	10	9	8	1967	5	4	3	2000	29	27	27
1935	29	27	27	1968	24	23	22	2001	19	17	17
1936	17	15	15	1969	12	11	10	2002	8	6	6
1937	6	4	4	1970	2	1	1/30	2003	27	26	25
1938	25	23	23	1971	20	19	19	2004	14	13	12
1939	15	13	12	1972	9	8	8	2005	4	3	2
1940	4	2	1/30	1973	28	27	26	2006	23	22	21
1941	22	21	20	1974	17	16	15	2007	13	12	11
1942	12	10	10	1975	7	5	5	2008	1/31	30	29
1943	1/30	29	29	1976	25	23	23	2009	20	19	18
1944	18	17	17	1977	14	13	12	2010	10	8	8
1945	8	6	6	1978	4	2	2/31	2011	29	27	27
1946	26	25	24	1979	22	21	20	2012	17	16	15

TABLE 2   MOON TABLE 3

DAY	SEP	OCT	M/D	X	Y	Z	a	b	d	e
1	X	a	0	VI	VI	LI	LI	LI	LI	SC
2	X	a	1	VI	LI	LI	LI	LI	SC	SC
3	X	a	2	LI	LI	LI	LI	SC	SC	SC
4	Y	b	3	LI	LI	SC	SC	SC	SC	SA
5	Y	b	4	LI	SC	SC	SC	SA	SA	SA
6	Y	b	5	SC	SC	SC	SA	SA	SA	CP
7	Y	b	6	SC	SA	SA	SA	CP	CP	CP
8	Y	b	7	SA	SA	SA	SA	CP	CP	AQ
9	Y	b	8	SA	SA	CP	CP	CP	CP	AQ
10	Y	b	9	SA	CP	CP	CP	AQ	AQ	AQ
11	Y	b	10	CP	CP	CP	AQ	AQ	AQ	PI
12	Y	b	11	CP	AQ	AQ	AQ	PI	PI	PI
13	Y	b	12	AQ	AQ	AQ	PI	PI	PI	AR
14	Z	d	13	AQ	AQ	PI	PI	AR	PI	AR
15	Z	d	14	PI	PI	PI	AR	AR	AR	TA
16	Z	d	15	PI	PI	PI	AR	AR	AR	TA
17	Z	d	16	PI	AR	AR	AR	AR	TA	TA
18	Z	d	17	AR	AR	AR	AR	TA	TA	GE
19	Z	d	18	AR	AR	AR	TA	TA	GE	GE
20	Z	d	19	AR	TA	TA	TA	TA	GE	GE
21	Z	d	20	TA	TA	TA	GE	GE	GE	CA
22	Z	d	21	TA	GE	GE	GE	GE	CA	CA
23	Z	d	22	GE	GE	GE	GE	CA	CA	CA
24	a	e	23	GE	GE	GE	CA	CA	CA	LE
25	a	e	24	GE	CA	CA	CA	CA	LE	LE
26	a	e	25	CA	CA	CA	CA	LE	LE	LE
27	a	e	26	CA	LE	LE	LE	LE	VI	VI
28	a	e	27	LE	LE	LE	LE	VI	VI	VI
29	a	e	28	LE	LE	LE	VI	VI	VI	LI
30	a	e	29	LE	VI	VI	VI	VI	LI	LI
31	–	e								

AR = Aries, TA = Taurus, GE = Gemini, CA = Cancer, LE = Leo, VI = Virgo,
LI = Libra, SC = Scorpio, SA = Sagittarius, CP = Capricorn, AQ = Aquarius, PI = Pisces

MOON SIGNS

Moon in Aries

You have a strong imagination, courage, determination and a desire to do things in your own way and forge your own path through life.

Originality is a key attribute; you are seldom stuck for ideas although your mind is changeable and you could take the time to focus on individual tasks. Often quick-tempered, you take orders from few people and live life at a fast pace. Avoid health problems by taking regular time out for rest and relaxation.

Emotionally, it is important that you talk to those you are closest to and work out your true feelings. Once you discover that people are there to help, there is less necessity for you to do everything yourself.

Moon in Taurus

The Moon in Taurus gives you a courteous and friendly manner, which means you are likely to have many friends.

The good things in life mean a lot to you, as Taurus is an Earth sign that delights in experiences which please the senses. Hence you are probably a lover of good food and drink, which may in turn mean you need to keep an eye on the bathroom scales, especially as looking good is also important to you.

Emotionally you are fairly stable and you stick by your own standards. Taureans do not respond well to change. Intuition also plays an important part in your life.

Moon in Gemini

You have a warm-hearted character, sympathetic and eager to help others. At times reserved, you can also be articulate and chatty: this is part of the paradox of Gemini, which always brings duplicity to the nature. You are interested in current affairs, have a good intellect, and are good company and likely to have many friends. Most of your friends have a high opinion of you and would be ready to defend you should the need arise. However, this is usually unnecessary, as you are quite capable of defending yourself in any verbal confrontation.

Travel is important to your inquisitive mind and you find intellectual stimulus in mixing with people from different cultures. You also gain much from reading, writing and the arts but you do need plenty of rest and relaxation in order to avoid fatigue.

Moon in Cancer

The Moon in Cancer at the time of birth is a fortunate position as Cancer is the Moon's natural home. This means that the qualities of compassion and understanding given by the Moon are especially enhanced in your nature, and you are friendly and sociable and cope well with emotional pressures. You cherish home and family life, and happily do the domestic tasks. Your surroundings are important to you and you hate squalor and filth. You are likely to have a love of music and poetry.

Your basic character, although at times changeable like the Moon itself, depends on symmetry. You aim to make your surroundings comfortable and harmonious, for yourself and those close to you.

Moon in Leo

The best qualities of the Moon and Leo come together to make you warm-hearted, fair, ambitious and self-confident. With good organisational abilities, you invariably rise to a position of responsibility in your chosen career. This is fortunate as you don't enjoy being an 'also-ran' and would rather be an important part of a small organisation than a menial in a large one.

You should be lucky in love, and happy, provided you put in the effort to make a comfortable home for yourself and those close to you. It is likely that you will have a love of pleasure, sport, music and literature. Life brings you many rewards, most of them as a direct result of your own efforts, although you may be luckier than average and ready to make the best of any situation.

Moon in Virgo

You are endowed with good mental abilities and a keen receptive memory, but you are never ostentatious or pretentious. Naturally quite reserved, you still have many friends, especially of the opposite sex. Marital relationships must be discussed carefully and worked at so that they remain harmonious, as personal attachments can be a problem if you do not give them your full attention.

Talented and persevering, you possess artistic qualities and are a good homemaker. Earning your honours through genuine merit, you work long and hard towards your objectives but show little pride in your achievements. Many short journeys will be undertaken in your life.

Moon in Libra

With the Moon in Libra you are naturally popular and make friends easily. People like you, probably more than you realise, you bring fun to a party and are a natural diplomat. For all its good points, Libra is not the most stable of astrological signs and, as a result, your emotions can be a little unstable too. Therefore, although the Moon in Libra is said to be good for love and marriage, your Sun sign and Rising sign will have an important effect on your emotional and loving qualities.

You must remember to relate to others in your decision-making. Co-operation is crucial because Libra represents the 'balance' of life that can only be achieved through harmonious relationships. Conformity is not easy for you because Libra, an Air sign, likes its independence.

Moon in Scorpio

Some people might call you pushy. In fact, all you really want to do is to live life to the full and protect yourself and your family from the pressures of life. Take care to avoid giving the impression of being sarcastic or impulsive and use your energies wisely and constructively.

You have great courage and you invariably achieve your goals by force of personality and sheer effort. You are fond of mystery and are good at predicting the outcome of situations and events. Travel experiences can be beneficial to you.

You may experience problems if you do not take time to examine your motives in a relationship, and also if you allow jealousy, always a feature of Scorpio, to cloud your judgement.

Moon in Sagittarius

The Moon in Sagittarius helps to make you a generous individual with humanitarian qualities and a kind heart. Restlessness may be intrinsic as your mind is seldom still. Perhaps because of this, you have a need for change that could lead you to several major moves during your adult life. You are not afraid to stand your ground when you know your judgement is right, you speak directly and have good intuition.

At work you are quick, efficient and versatile and so you make an ideal employee. You need work to be intellectually demanding and do not enjoy tedious routines.

In relationships, you anger quickly if faced with stupidity or deception, though you are just as quick to forgive and forget. Emotionally, there are times when your heart rules your head.

Moon in Capricorn

The Moon in Capricorn makes you popular and likely to come into the public eye in some way. The watery Moon is not entirely comfortable in the Earth sign of Capricorn and this may lead to some difficulties in the early years of life. An initial lack of creative ability and indecision must be overcome before the true qualities of patience and perseverance inherent in Capricorn can show through.

You have good administrative ability and are a capable worker, and if you are careful you can accumulate wealth. But you must be cautious and take professional advice in partnerships, as you are open to deception. You may be interested in social or welfare work, which suit your organisational skills and sympathy for others.

Moon in Aquarius

The Moon in Aquarius makes you an active and agreeable person with a friendly, easy-going nature. Sympathetic to the needs of others, you flourish in a laid-back atmosphere. You are broad-minded, fair and open to suggestion, although sometimes you have an unconventional quality which others can find hard to understand.

You are interested in the strange and curious, and in old articles and places. You enjoy trips to these places and gain much from them. Political, scientific and educational work interests you and you might choose a career in science or technology.

Money-wise, you make gains through innovation and concentration and Lunar Aquarians often tackle more than one job at a time. In love you are kind and honest.

Moon in Pisces

You have a kind, sympathetic nature, somewhat retiring at times, but you always take account of others' feelings and help when you can.

Personal relationships may be problematic, but as life goes on you can learn from your experiences and develop a better understanding of yourself and the world around you.

You have a fondness for travel, appreciate beauty and harmony and hate disorder and strife. You may be fond of literature and would make a good writer or speaker yourself. You have a creative imagination and may come across as an incurable romantic. You have strong intuition, maybe bordering on a mediumistic quality, which sets you apart from the mass. You may not be rich in cash terms, but your personal gifts are worth more than gold.

LIBRA IN LOVE

Discover how compatible you are with people from the same and other signs of the zodiac. Five stars equals a match made in heaven!

Libra meets Libra

This is a potentially successful match because Librans are extremely likeable people, and so it stands to reason that two Librans together will be twice as pleasant and twice as much fun. However, Librans can also be indecisive and need an anchor from which to find practical and financial success, and obviously one Libran won't provide this for another. Librans can be flighty in a romantic sense, so both parties will need to develop a steadfast approach for a long-term relationship. Star rating: ****

Libra meets Scorpio

Many astrologers have reservations about this match because, on the surface, the signs are so different. However, this couple may find fulfilment because these differences mean that their respective needs are met. Scorpio needs a partner to lighten the load which won't daunt Libra, while Libra looks for a steadfast quality which it doesn't possess, but Scorpio can supply naturally. Financial success is possible because they both have good ideas and back them up with hard work and determination. All in all, a promising outlook. Star rating: ****

Libra meets Sagittarius

Libra and Sagittarius are both adaptable signs who get on well with most people, but this promising outlook often does not follow through because each brings out the flighty side of the other. This combination is great for a fling, but when the romance is over someone needs to see to the practical side of life. Both signs are well meaning, pleasant and kind, but are either of them constant enough to build a life together? In at least some of the cases, the answer would be no. Star rating: ***

Libra meets Capricorn

Libra and Capricorn rub each other up the wrong way because their attitudes to life are so different, and although both are capable of doing something about this, in reality they probably won't. Capricorn is steady, determined and solid, while Libra is bright but sometimes superficial and not entirely reliable. They usually lack the instant spark needed to get them together in the first place, so when it does happen it is often because one of the partners is not typical of their sign. Star rating: **

Libra meets Aquarius

One of the best combinations imaginable, partly because both are Air signs and so share a common meeting point. But perhaps the more crucial factor is that both signs respect each other. Aquarius loves life and originality, and is quite intellectual. Libra is similar, but more balanced and rather less eccentric. A visit to this couple's house would be entertaining and full of zany wit, activity and excitement. Both are keen to travel and may prefer to 'find themselves' before taking on too many domestic responsibilities. Star rating: *****

Libra meets Pisces

Libra and Pisces can be extremely fond of each other, even deeply in love, but this alone isn't a stable foundation for long-term success. Pisces is extremely deep and doesn't even know itself very well. Libra may initially find this intriguing but will eventually feel frustrated at being unable to understand the Piscean's emotional and personal feelings. Pisces can be jealous and may find Libra's flightiness difficult, which Libra can't stand. They are great friends and they may make it to the romantic stakes, but when they get there a lot of effort will be necessary. Star rating: ***

Libra meets Aries

These are zodiac opposites which means a make-or-break situation. The match will either be a great success or a dismal failure. Why? Well, Aries finds it difficult to understand the flighty Air-sign tendencies of Libra, whilst the natural balance of Libra contradicts the unorthodox Arian methods. Any flexibility will come from Libra, which may mean that things work out for a while, but Libra only has so much patience and it may eventually run out. In the end, Aries may be just too bossy for an independent but sensitive sign like Libra. Star rating: **

Libra meets Taurus

A happy life is important to both these signs and, as they are both ruled by Venus, they share a common understanding, even though they display themselves so differently. Taurus is quieter than Libra, but can be decisive, and that's what counts. Libra is interested in absolutely everything, an infectious quality when seen through Taurean eyes. The slightly flighty qualities of Libra may lead to jealousy from the Bull. Not an argumentative relationship and one that often works well. There could be many changes of address for this pair. Star rating: ****

Libra meets Gemini

One of the best possible zodiac combinations. Libra and Gemini are both Air signs, which leads to a meeting of minds. Both signs simply love to have a good time, although Libra is the tidiest and less forgetful. Gemini's capricious nature won't bother Libra, who acts as a stabilising influence. Life should generally run smoothly, and any rows are likely to be short and sharp. Both parties genuinely like each other, which is of paramount importance in a relationship and, ultimately, there isn't a better reason for being or staying together. Star rating: *****

Libra meets Cancer

Almost anyone can get on with Libra, which is one of the most adaptable signs of them all. But being adaptable does not always lead to fulfilment and a successful match here will require a quiet Libran and a slightly more progressive Cancerian than the norm. Both signs are pleasant and polite, and like domestic order, but Libra may find Cancer too emotional and perhaps lacking in vibrancy, while Libra, on the other hand, may be a little too flighty for steady Cancer. Star rating: ***

Libra meets Leo

The biggest drawback here is likely to be in the issue of commitment. Leo knows everything about constancy and faithfulness, a lesson which, sadly, Libra needs to learn. Librans are easy-going and diplomatic, qualities which are useful when Leo is on the war-path. This couple should be compatible on a personal level and any problems tend to relate to the different way in which these signs deal with outside factors. With good will and an open mind, it can work out well enough. Star rating: ***

Libra meets Virgo

There have been some rare occasions when this match has found great success, but usually the darker and more inward-looking Virgoan depresses the naturally gregarious Libran. Libra appears self-confident, but is not so beneath the surface, and needs encouragement to develop inner confidence, which may not come from Virgo. Constancy can be a problem for Libra, who also tires easily and may find Virgo dull. A lighter, less serious approach to life from Virgo is needed to make this work. Star rating: **

VENUS:
THE PLANET OF LOVE

If you look up at the sky around sunset or sunrise you will often see Venus in close attendance to the Sun. It is arguably one of the most beautiful sights of all and there is little wonder that historically it became associated with the goddess of love. But although Venus does play an important part in the way you view love and in the way others see you romantically, this is only one of the spheres of influence that it enjoys in your overall character.

Venus has a part to play in the more cultured side of your life and has much to do with your appreciation of art, literature, music and general creativity. Even the way you look is responsive to the part of the zodiac that Venus occupied at the start of your life, though this fact is also down to your Sun sign and Ascending sign. If, at the time you were born, Venus occupied one of the more gregarious zodiac signs, you will be more likely to wear your heart on your sleeve, as well as to be more attracted to entertainment, social gatherings and good company. If on the other hand Venus occupied a quiet zodiac sign at the time of your birth, you would tend to be more retiring and less willing to shine in public situations.

It's good to know what part the planet Venus plays in your life for it can have a great bearing on the way you appear to the rest of the world and since we all have to mix with others, you can learn to make the very best of what Venus has to offer you.

One of the great complications in the past has always been trying to establish exactly what zodiac position Venus enjoyed when you were born because the planet is notoriously difficult to track. However, we have solved that problem by creating a table that is exclusive to your Sun sign, which you will find on the following page.

Establishing your Venus sign could not be easier. Just look up the year of your birth on the next page and you will see a sign of the zodiac. This was the sign that Venus occupied in the period covered by your sign in that year. If Venus occupied more than one sign during the period, this is indicated by the date on which the sign changed, and the name of the new sign. For instance, if you were born in 1950, Venus was in Virgo until the 4th October, after which time it was in Libra. If you were born before 4th October your Venus sign is Virgo, if you were born on or after 4th October, your Venus sign is Libra. Once you have established the position of Venus at the time of your birth, you can then look in the pages which follow to see how this has a bearing on your life as a whole.

1914 SCORPIO / 10.10 SAGITTARIUS
1915 LIBRA / 16.10 SCORPIO
1916 LEO / 8.10 VIRGO
1917 SCORPIO / 12.10 SAGITTARIUS
1918 VIRGO / 6.10 LIBRA
1919 SCORPIO / 12.10 SAGITTARIUS
1920 LIBRA / 30.9 SCORPIO
1921 LEO / 26.9 VIRGO /
    21.10 LIBRA
1922 SCORPIO / 11.10 SAGITTARIUS
1923 LIBRA / 16.10 SCORPIO
1924 LEO / 8.10 VIRGO
1925 SCORPIO / 12.10 SAGITTARIUS
1926 VIRGO / 6.10 LIBRA
1927 VIRGO
1928 LIBRA / 29.9 SCORPIO
1929 LEO / 26.9 VIRGO /
    20.10 LIBRA
1930 SCORPIO / 12.10 SAGITTARIUS
1931 LIBRA / 15.10 SCORPIO
1932 LEO / 7.10 VIRGO
1933 SCORPIO / 11.10 SAGITTARIUS
1934 VIRGO / 5.10 LIBRA
1935 VIRGO
1936 LIBRA / 28.9 SCORPIO
1937 LEO / 25.9 VIRGO /
    20.10 LIBRA
1938 SCORPIO / 14.10 SAGITTARIUS
1939 LIBRA / 14.10 SCORPIO
1940 LEO / 7.10 VIRGO
1941 SCORPIO / 11.10 SAGITTARIUS
1942 VIRGO / 5.10 LIBRA
1943 VIRGO
1944 LIBRA / 28.9 SCORPIO
1945 LEO / 25.9 VIRGO /
    19.10 LIBRA
1946 SCORPIO / 14.10 SAGITTARIUS
1947 LIBRA / 13.10 SCORPIO
1948 LEO / 7.10 VIRGO
1949 SCORPIO / 11.10 SAGITTARIUS
1950 VIRGO / 4.10 LIBRA
1951 VIRGO
1952 LIBRA / 27.9 SCORPIO
1953 VIRGO / 19.10 LIBRA
1954 SCORPIO / 16.10 SAGITTARIUS
1955 SCORPIO / 12.10 SCORPIO
1956 LEO / 6.10 VIRGO
1957 SCORPIO / 10.10 SAGITTARIUS
1958 VIRGO / 4.10 LIBRA
1959 VIRGO / 28.9 LEO
1960 LIBRA / 27.9 SCORPIO
1961 VIRGO / 18.10 LIBRA
1962 SCORPIO / 16.10 SAGITTARIUS
1963 LIBRA / 12.10 SCORPIO

1964 LEO / 6.10 VIRGO
1965 SCORPIO / 9.10 SAGITTARIUS
1966 VIRGO / 4.10 LIBRA
1967 VIRGO / 3.10 LEO
1968 LIBRA / 26.9 SCORPIO
1969 VIRGO / 17.10 LIBRA
1970 SCORPIO / 19.10 SAGITTARIUS
1971 LIBRA / 11.10 SCORPIO
1972 LEO / 6.10 VIRGO
1973 SCORPIO / 9.10 SAGITTARIUS
1974 VIRGO / 3.10 LIBRA
1975 VIRGO / 5.10 LEO
1976 LIBRA / 26.9 SCORPIO
1977 VIRGO / 17.10 LIBRA
1978 SCORPIO / 19.10 SAGITTARIUS
1979 LIBRA / 11.10 SCORPIO
1980 LEO / 5.10 VIRGO
1981 SCORPIO / 9.10 SAGITTARIUS
1982 VIRGO / 3.10 LIBRA
1983 VIRGO / 7.10 LEO
1984 LIBRA / 25.9 SCORPIO
1985 VIRGO / 16.10 LIBRA
1986 SCORPIO
1987 LIBRA / 10.10 SCORPIO
1988 LEO / 5.10 VIRGO
1989 SCORPIO / 8.10 SAGITTARIUS
1990 VIRGO / 2.10 LIBRA
1991 VIRGO / 8.10 LEO
1992 LIBRA / 25.9 SCORPIO
1993 VIRGO / 16.10 LIBRA
1994 SCORPIO
1995 LIBRA / 10.10 SCORPIO
1996 LEO / 5.10 VIRGO
1997 SCORPIO / 8.10 SAGITTARIUS
1998 VIRGO / 2.10 LIBRA
1999 VIRGO / 9.10 LEO
2000 LIBRA / 25.9 SCORPIO
2001 LEO / 5.10 VIRGO
2002 SCORPIO / 8.10 SAGITTARIUS
2003 LIBRA / 10.10 SCORPIO
2004 LEO / 5.10 VIRGO
2005 SCORPIO / 8.10 SAGITTARIUS
2006 VIRGO / 2.10 LIBRA
2007 VIRGO / 9.10 LEO
2008 LIBRA / 25.9 SCORPIO
2009 LEO / 5.10 VIRGO
2010 SCORPIO / 8.10 SAGITTARIUS
2011 LIBRA / 10.10 SCORPIO
2012 LEO / 5.10 VIRGO

VENUS THROUGH THE ZODIAC SIGNS

Venus in Aries

Amongst other things, the position of Venus in Aries indicates a fondness for travel, music and all creative pursuits. Your nature tends to be affectionate and you would try not to create confusion or difficulty for others if it could be avoided. Many people with this planetary position have a great love of the theatre, and mental stimulation is of the greatest importance. Early romantic attachments are common with Venus in Aries, so it is very important to establish a genuine sense of romantic continuity. Early marriage is not recommended, especially if it is based on sympathy. You may give your heart a little too readily on occasions.

Venus in Taurus

You are capable of very deep feelings and your emotions tend to last for a very long time. This makes you a trusting partner and lover, whose constancy is second to none. In life you are precise and careful and always try to do things the right way. Although this means an ordered life, which you are comfortable with, it can also lead you to be rather too fussy for your own good. Despite your pleasant nature, you are very fixed in your opinions and quite able to speak your mind. Others are attracted to you and historical astrologers always quoted this position of Venus as being very fortunate in terms of marriage. However, if you find yourself involved in a failed relationship, it could take you a long time to trust again.

Venus in Gemini

As with all associations related to Gemini, you tend to be quite versatile, anxious for change and intelligent in your dealings with the world at large. You may gain money from more than one source but you are equally good at spending it. There is an inference here that you are a good communicator, via either the written or the spoken word, and you love to be in the company of interesting people. Always on the look-out for culture, you may also be very fond of music, and love to indulge the curious and cultured side of your nature. In romance you tend to have more than one relationship and could find yourself associated with someone who has previously been a friend or even a distant relative.

Venus in Cancer

You often stay close to home because you are very fond of family and enjoy many of your most treasured moments when you are with those you love. Being naturally sympathetic, you will always do anything you can to support those around you, even people you hardly know at all. This charitable side of your nature is your most noticeable trait and is one of the reasons why others are naturally so fond of you. Being receptive and in some cases even psychic, you can see through to the soul of most of those with whom you come into contact. You may not commence too many romantic attachments but when you do give your heart, it tends to be unconditionally.

Venus in Leo

It must become quickly obvious to almost anyone you meet that you are kind, sympathetic and yet determined enough to stand up for anyone or anything that is truly important to you. Bright and sunny, you warm the world with your natural enthusiasm and would rarely do anything to hurt those around you, or at least not intentionally. In romance you are ardent and sincere, though some may find your style just a little overpowering. Gains come through your contacts with other people and this could be especially true with regard to romance, for love and money often come hand in hand for those who were born with Venus in Leo. People claim to understand you, though you are more complex than you seem.

Venus in Virgo

Your nature could well be fairly quiet no matter what your Sun sign might be, though this fact often manifests itself as an inner peace and would not prevent you from being basically sociable. Some delays and even the odd disappointment in love cannot be ruled out with this planetary position, though it's a fact that you will usually find the happiness you look for in the end. Catapulting yourself into romantic entanglements that you know to be rather ill-advised is not sensible, and it would be better to wait before you committed yourself exclusively to any one person. It is the essence of your nature to serve the world at large and through doing so it is possible that you will attract money at some stage in your life.

Venus in Libra

Venus is very comfortable in Libra and bestows upon those people who have this planetary position a particular sort of kindness that is easy to recognise. This is a very good position for all sorts of friendships and also for romantic attachments that usually bring much joy into your life. Few individuals with Venus in Libra would avoid marriage and since you are capable of great depths of love, it is likely that you will find a contented personal life. You like to mix with people of integrity and intelligence but don't take kindly to scruffy surroundings or work that means getting your hands too dirty. Careful speculation, good business dealings and money through marriage all seem fairly likely.

Venus in Scorpio

You are quite open and tend to spend money quite freely, even on those occasions when you don't have very much. Although your intentions are always good, there are times when you get yourself in to the odd scrape and this can be particularly true when it comes to romance, which you may come to late or from a rather unexpected direction. Certainly you have the power to be happy and to make others contented on the way, but you find the odd stumbling block on your journey through life and it could seem that you have to work harder than those around you. As a result of this, you gain a much deeper understanding of the true value of personal happiness than many people ever do, and are likely to achieve true contentment in the end.

Venus in Sagittarius

You are lighthearted, cheerful and always able to see the funny side of any situation. These facts enhance your popularity, which is especially high with members of the opposite sex. You should never have to look too far to find romantic interest in your life, though it is just possible that you might be too willing to commit yourself before you are certain that the person in question is right for you. Part of the problem here extends to other areas of life too. The fact is that you like variety in everything and so can tire of situations that fail to offer it. All the same, if you choose wisely and learn to understand your restless side, then great happiness can be yours.

Venus in Capricorn

The most notable trait that comes from Venus in this position is that it makes you trustworthy and able to take on all sorts of responsibilities in life. People are instinctively fond of you and love you all the more because you are always ready to help those who are in any form of need. Social and business popularity can be yours and there is a magnetic quality to your nature that is particularly attractive in a romantic sense. Anyone who wants a partner for a lover, a spouse and a good friend too would almost certainly look in your direction. Constancy is the hallmark of your nature and unfaithfulness would go right against the grain. You might sometimes be a little too trusting.

Venus in Aquarius

This location of Venus offers a fondness for travel and a desire to try out something new at every possible opportunity. You are extremely easy to get along with and tend to have many friends from varied backgrounds, classes and inclinations. You like to live a distinct sort of life and gain a great deal from moving about, both in a career sense and with regard to your home. It is not out of the question that you could form a romantic attachment to someone who comes from far away or be attracted to a person of a distinctly artistic and original nature. What you cannot stand is jealousy, for you have friends of both sexes and would want to keep things that way.

Venus in Pisces

The first thing people tend to notice about you is your wonderful, warm smile. Being very charitable by nature you will do anything to help others, even if you don't know them well. Much of your life may be spent sorting out situations for other people, but it is very important to feel that you are living for yourself too. In the main, you remain cheerful, and tend to be quite attractive to members of the opposite sex. Where romantic attachments are concerned, you could be drawn to people who are significantly older or younger than yourself or to someone with a unique career or point of view. It might be best for you to avoid marrying whilst you are still very young.

LIBRA:
2011 DIARY PAGES

October
2011

1 SATURDAY
Moon Age Day 4   Moon Sign Scorpio

It isn't a matter of being the best team player this weekend, but more about your ability to persuade other people to follow your lead. You can't expect everyone's views to accord with your own thinking, even if these are opinions expressed by friends. If you can't bring them round, you might have to go it alone.

2 SUNDAY
Moon Age Day 5   Moon Sign Sagittarius

Energy definitely shouldn't be lacking, and the present position of the Sun encourages you to be more of a go-getter than ever. You can be a fund of laughter and jokes at this time, and can use this trend to boost your popularity. There isn't anything unusual about that, except for its intensity. Some Librans could be fighting off admirers now!

3 MONDAY
Moon Age Day 6   Moon Sign Sagittarius

Communications can work very favourably for you today and you need to bear in mind that if you want something, this is the best time of the year to go out and ask for it. Even if you think your requests are outrageous, people can only say no. But there's no harm in using your skills to try to persuade them to help you out.

4 TUESDAY
Moon Age Day 7   Moon Sign Sagittarius

This would be an ideal time for making small changes to your family life, assisted by a combination of the Sun and Moon. None of these are likely to be sweeping or problematical, and in the main you should be jogging along quite happily. At work you might decide to alter the status quo or to take on a different sort of responsibility.

5 WEDNESDAY   *Moon Age Day 8   Moon Sign Capricorn*

Your self-determined approach to life at this time may well prove infectious to others. The problem arises if you inspire some people to do things for which they are definitely not equipped. There's nothing to stop you lending a hand if necessary. Life could well be a doddle for most Libran subjects right now.

6 THURSDAY   *Moon Age Day 9   Moon Sign Capricorn*

It is entirely possible that you could overstep the mark in a romantic situation today. Being confident is all very well, though you need to ask yourself whether you are going slightly too far. The current interlude works best if you are modest and unassuming, because that's the way most people want to see you.

7 FRIDAY   *Moon Age Day 10   Moon Sign Aquarius*

Your appeal and your personal magnetism certainly shouldn't be in doubt whilst the Sun and Venus are in your solar first house. Confidence reigns supreme in most situations, and you have what it takes to be the king or queen in most social settings. If there is a problem today, it could be that you are pushing yourself slightly too hard.

8 SATURDAY   *Moon Age Day 11   Moon Sign Aquarius*

Diplomacy is the name of the game today, because in your desire to show how positive and dynamic you are, there's a risk of you overlooking some of the niceties of life. Don't worry about the odd mistake, because you can win others around with your charm. In fact, perhaps under current influences you could get away with anything!

9 SUNDAY   *Moon Age Day 12   Moon Sign Aquarius*

This is definitely a period of power and a time to flex your muscles in order to get things working in the direction you think is best. Even if you weren't planning to be out there at the head of the pack, it's where you rightfully belong. Rather than agonising over romantic decisions, just be prepared to do what you know is right.

10 MONDAY
Moon Age Day 13   Moon Sign Pisces

You can get the best out of today by being very chatty and willing to get involved in almost any type of conversations. It's important that you know what you like at the moment and that you follow your own ideas as much as possible. Most important of all, you ought to be using your charm to get other people to follow your reasoning.

11 TUESDAY
Moon Age Day 14   Moon Sign Pisces

This may turn out to be a 'treading water' sort of phase. The lunar low comes along tomorrow, so you need to ask yourself whether there is any real point in starting anything new and startling. What you can do is to finalise details for later, get things in order in a general sense and think about your intended path across the next few weeks.

12 WEDNESDAY
Moon Age Day 15   Moon Sign Aries

Any new responsibilities that are on offer now might have to wait until you are in a more positive period. The lunar low encourages you to keep things at arm's length and not to make major decisions unless you are forced to do so. Unexpected situations are a distinct possibility, so try to prepare yourself for them but don't over-react.

13 THURSDAY
Moon Age Day 16   Moon Sign Aries

Social situations are not particularly well accented today, and you might choose to retreat into yourself if it proves possible to do so. Extra effort will be required if you decide to mix with an unfamiliar crowd, which is possible, but could be quite tiring. By tomorrow the positive trends return and you should be feeling more like yourself.

14 FRIDAY
Moon Age Day 17   Moon Sign Taurus

Leisure pursuits are all very well, but you need to consider the demands they make on your pocket. Do you have the necessary resources to participate? Maybe you could turn your ingenious mind to thinking about what you can save, and where. Friendship has potential to be especially important around this time.

15 SATURDAY   *Moon Age Day 18   Moon Sign Taurus*

The Sun in your solar first house helps you to find inspiration to tackle any jobs you have been avoiding. You can afford to get involved, even in projects that haven't been going too well of late. In fact, you might be able to breathe new life into something that had seemed dead in the water.

16 SUNDAY   *Moon Age Day 19   Moon Sign Gemini*

Travel comes under the spotlight now, and so you should be willing to go anywhere, even at a moment's notice. You have a chance to enjoy the cut and thrust of life whilst the Sun occupies its present position, and you can use this trend to ring the changes in your daily routines. It's also time to try to ease any recent pressures at home.

17 MONDAY   *Moon Age Day 20   Moon Sign Gemini*

There are signs that setbacks could dog you in terms of friendships, particularly if you are taking yourself too much for granted. It's important to realise how important you are to those around you, and to allow them to 'prove' their commitment. Be prepared to stand back while they do so.

18 TUESDAY   *Moon Age Day 21   Moon Sign Gemini*

There is a good boost on offer in terms of professional developments, and this might even include a very pleasant surprise at work. However, you also need to be aware that not everyone may be quite as committed to doing things properly as you are, so there's much to be said for checking the work of other people.

19 WEDNESDAY   *Moon Age Day 22   Moon Sign Cancer*

Money-wise you should now be bringing things together quite nicely. If it feels as though you are short of cash, maybe it's time to think about all the different sources of money you have access to. Looking at the situation honestly might show you that things are better than you thought. It pays to keep a weather eye on family spending.

20 THURSDAY   *Moon Age Day 23   Moon Sign Cancer*

Social relationships now function best when you cultivate that helpful spirit for which Libra is so famous. It's a question of showing people how caring and kind you can be, as well as being inspirational and funny. If you do have any problems today, why not find someone who can be persuaded to lend you a helping hand?

21 FRIDAY   *Moon Age Day 24   Moon Sign Leo*

Economic issues now come to the fore, and even if you are quite happy with the way things are going in a general sense, there's a chance you could be feeling slightly less well off than you hoped. It's sensible to tackle your finances head-on, though there is little to be gained from panicking. The planets can be very supportive at this time.

22 SATURDAY   *Moon Age Day 25   Moon Sign Leo*

The material side of life and the little luxuries you can obtain could well put a smile on your face this weekend. The fact is that you are in a position to spoil yourself and to persuade other people to contribute too. There's much to be said for putting on your best clothes and getting out of the house to party!

23 SUNDAY   *Moon Age Day 26   Moon Sign Virgo*

Inspiration is fine, but do make sure that you don't get carried away with your enthusiasm on this particular Sunday. Your best approach is to take a realistic view of the skills you possess and to act sensibly, while making the most of positive planetary trends. Knowledge and experience seem to be the keys to success now.

24 MONDAY   *Moon Age Day 27   Moon Sign Virgo*

This is a favourable time on the whole for settling any outstanding financial issues. You may even be able to get things into order that you have failed to do for the last few weeks or even months. There is an emphasis on making sense of situations and getting them to fall into place. Your tidy mind should help you no end.

25 TUESDAY
Moon Age Day 28   Moon Sign Libra

Getting an early start can make all the difference today. The lunar high is offering all sorts of incentives that weren't obvious before. You can tap into plenty of energy, a great deal of ingenuity and a strong desire to get things done. What's even more important is that natural good luck is on your side – always a good sign.

26 WEDNESDAY
Moon Age Day 29   Moon Sign Libra

Jobs that would have taken you ages to complete last week can now be done in a flash. You may even surprise yourself with how much you get through, and you can afford to end the day feeling happy with your achievements. It's time to put delays and difficulties behind you, though family members could still cause a little irritation.

27 THURSDAY
Moon Age Day 0   Moon Sign Scorpio

Trends assist you to focus far better and more firmly on creating a secure financial base, something you have probably been trying to do for days or weeks. There should be less uncertainty about now, and although the lunar high has gone, a second-house Sun gives you every encouragement to think clearly and act in your own best interests.

28 FRIDAY
Moon Age Day 1   Moon Sign Scorpio

Venus has now moved into your solar second house, and so the finer things of life are yours for the taking. This is a great position for Venus as far as you are concerned because it allows the more cultured side of your nature room to move. A day to avoid anything that seems vulgar or common and to show yourself to the world at your best.

29 SATURDAY
Moon Age Day 2   Moon Sign Sagittarius

Progress is possible in terms of personal objectives, and this weekend could give you the chance to socialise more. If you have been busy with work throughout most of the week, you can afford to take some time to yourself. Any headaches tend to be caused by worries regarding family members.

30 SUNDAY *Moon Age Day 3   Moon Sign Sagittarius*

Financial and business talks are well accented, though of course these might have to take second place on a Sunday. Even if this is the case, you can still sort things out and take great delight in doing so. Be careful you don't get ahead of yourself in some respects, because there is a slight chance of some unforced errors.

31 MONDAY *Moon Age Day 4   Moon Sign Capricorn*

The last day of the month offers some new incentives and once again assists you to firm up your resources ahead of the end of the year. Unpleasant surprises are a natural aspect of life, but if you remain in a positive frame of mind right now you can even turn these to your advantage. Look for the best in life and you will find it.

November 2011

1 TUESDAY
Moon Age Day 5   Moon Sign Capricorn

It's time to turn your thoughts towards inner emotions. The Moon in your solar fourth house encourages you to muse about family matters and maybe find reasons to agitate over the way family members are behaving. A quiet word in the right ear might be all you need to put things right, so don't stay silent about things you know should be discussed.

2 WEDNESDAY
Moon Age Day 6   Moon Sign Aquarius

Joint finances can now be dealt with, and even if there are some distractions around today, in the main you have what it takes to keep your eye on the ball. Arguments in social settings are best avoided, and it's not worth taking sides unless you feel really strongly about something. Be ready to show people how even-handed and impartial you can be.

3 THURSDAY
Moon Age Day 7   Moon Sign Aquarius

A dynamic and self-assertive approach is the order of the day, which may surprise a few people and could even shock you. Your strength lies in your willingness to come down positively in very specific ways, perhaps even about things that often confuse you. Libra is sometimes accused of sitting on the fence, but you shouldn't be doing so today.

4 FRIDAY
Moon Age Day 8   Moon Sign Aquarius

Progress today is about taking the initiative far more than usual. You have scope to be more productive at work, and you shouldn't have any problem dealing with a host of situations, all at the same time. You can certainly impress others with your ability to hold so much in your head, but being a Libran subject you've probably been making lists.

5 SATURDAY
Moon Age Day 9   Moon Sign Pisces

Another potentially productive period, especially when it comes to your finances. You have good reasoning powers, excellent recall, and a willingness to be very specific about everything. Don't be surprised if this comes as a shock to certain individuals who are more accustomed to you seeing all sides of any particular argument.

6 SUNDAY
Moon Age Day 10   Moon Sign Pisces

Energy and personal magnetism are highlighted, and although the lunar low is just around the corner you are unlikely to register the fact today. On the contrary, everything is about activity, and your positive approach can work wonders. Capitalise on the chance to boost your popularity.

7 MONDAY
Moon Age Day 11   Moon Sign Aries

With the lunar low around you may not be feeling on top of the world at the beginning of this week, particularly if you are starting to notice that winter is upon us. If you want to make this a cheerful day you will have to put in some extra effort. Try to find some humour in everyday situations, and retain your usual optimism.

8 TUESDAY
Moon Age Day 12   Moon Sign Aries

Swimming against the tide is sometimes a waste of time, so you might allow yourself to go with it today. Any problems are likely to be temporary, and you should be able to garner some assistance if you need it. Confidence might be hard to find, and there are good reasons to check and re-check details before committing yourself to anything.

9 WEDNESDAY
Moon Age Day 13   Moon Sign Aries

With the present position of the Sun this could be a good time for strengthening your finances and for using the resources you presently have more wisely. Look for new ventures on the horizon, especially with regard to work, and be prepared to help others find just the right solution to any problems they are encountering now.

10 THURSDAY   *Moon Age Day 14   Moon Sign Taurus*

Your reactions at this time are like quicksilver, and this can assist you to put yourself at the forefront of events. Any shyness that was present at the beginning of the week can now be dispelled, and you have what it takes to show a great sense of purpose and perseverance. Any delays early in the day can be quickly overcome.

11 FRIDAY   *Moon Age Day 15   Moon Sign Taurus*

You can get on well with everyone today – though there's nothing remotely remarkable about that for the average Libran subject. Confidence should be generally high, and your love life in particular is well accented. You can now afford to consider taking a little risk with regard to a particular venture.

12 SATURDAY   *Moon Age Day 16   Moon Sign Gemini*

There are signs that not everything you assume to be true turns out to be so, and today offers you a short interlude to re-think your strategies and to look at things in a different light. This is a time to back your own hunches, even if other people tell you that you are wrong. With perseverance you can easily prove a point today.

13 SUNDAY   *Moon Age Day 17   Moon Sign Gemini*

Use your relentless energy and masses of drive to give a much-needed boost to life. You have a good ability to cope when under pressure, some of which you might be creating for yourself in any case. Make sure you have something special to look forward to this evening, even if it's just a television programme you've been waiting for!

14 MONDAY   *Moon Age Day 18   Moon Sign Gemini*

An increase in enthusiasm enables you to remain energetic, active and willing to take on more and more in the way of responsibility. This would be an ideal time to welcome people you don't see very often back into your life, or to get in touch with someone who lives at a distance. If routines are boring, why not do something about them?

15 TUESDAY   *Moon Age Day 19   Moon Sign Cancer*

Venus is now in your solar third house. This is a positive influence that should assist you in gathering useful information. Even if you don't get on as well in a practical sense as you would wish, any slight mistakes you make can be the source of great amusement, both for you and for others. You certainly don't lack charm right now.

16 WEDNESDAY   *Moon Age Day 20   Moon Sign Cancer*

Trends indicate an element of self-deception at this time, and you need to be especially careful to check things carefully before you proceed in any new direction. There may well be people who want to be of assistance, but do they really know what they are doing? In the end you are better off making your own decisions and staying self-reliant.

17 THURSDAY   *Moon Age Day 21   Moon Sign Leo*

Work hard and play hard – that's a suitable motto for today. The Sun remains in a very positive position for you and there should be plenty to write home about at the moment. However, the one thing you need to avoid is self-indulgence. It's OK to spoil yourself now and again, but there's a risk of you going overboard at this time.

18 FRIDAY   *Moon Age Day 22   Moon Sign Leo*

An enterprising outlook is the order of the day, and you shouldn't find it difficult to change direction at a moment's notice if it proves to be possible. This would be a good time to improve yourself in some way – perhaps taking up some new hobby or beginning to study a new subject. Libra is on a roll, and there's no doubting the fact.

19 SATURDAY   *Moon Age Day 23   Moon Sign Virgo*

Don't be at all surprised if there is an element of confusion around today. It isn't that you fail to realise what you should be doing, it's just that things have potential to go wrong in more than one way. All of this should be more of a cause for amusement than annoyance, especially if you remain in a happy and positive frame of mind.

20 SUNDAY   *Moon Age Day 24   Moon Sign Virgo*

An influence comes along right now that assists you in all financial matters. Progress might not be possible all at once, and you shouldn't expect any fanfare, but there isn't much doubt that you should be, in some way, better off soon. Relying on the loyalty and support of friends is fine, though beware a tendency to do it a little too much.

21 MONDAY   *Moon Age Day 25   Moon Sign Virgo*

The Moon is now in your solar twelfth house, encouraging you to be slightly quieter for a few hours. This is not a trend that is likely to last long and by tomorrow the lunar high will assist you to catapult yourself back into the spotlight. For now you can afford to take a rest and enjoy watching rather than taking part.

22 TUESDAY   *Moon Age Day 26   Moon Sign Libra*

Spirits and motivation run high as you realise just what you are capable of doing. The lunar high assists you to find plenty of laughter throughout the day, and you have potential to keep everyone around you amused. The only fly in the ointment could be a tendency to believe that you are making a fool of yourself, which is not the case.

23 WEDNESDAY   *Moon Age Day 27   Moon Sign Libra*

An energetic and competitive approach continues to be the key for some of the challenges you choose to take on during the middle of this week. With one eye firmly on the end of the year already, you might decide to do some Christmas shopping, and this could be a chance to show the most cheerful and devil-may-care attitude to the world.

24 THURSDAY   ☿   *Moon Age Day 28   Moon Sign Scorpio*

Now the Sun has moved into your solar third house and this allows you to feel more mentally alert. You should be keeping your thinking processes clear, and ensuring you don't forget things. Rather than taking friends for granted right now, be happy to help out if it proves to be possible. This even applies to the odd pest!

25 FRIDAY ☿ *Moon Age Day 0   Moon Sign Scorpio*

It might seem difficult to retain control over every single aspect of your life, but do you really need to do so? If you allow other people to do what they think is right for you, you could be quite surprised at the result. Creature comforts may seem more inviting than they have done recently, maybe as a result of the onset of winter.

26 SATURDAY ☿ *Moon Age Day 1   Moon Sign Sagittarius*

Certain social acquaintances may prove to be highly useful to your overall path through life this weekend. You can even persuade people you haven't been particularly close to in the past to play a much more important part in your life. Keep your eyes and ears open for new input today, no matter what you happen to be doing.

27 SUNDAY ☿ *Moon Age Day 2   Moon Sign Sagittarius*

It's possible you could enjoy a less demanding day today, partly because the Moon is in your solar fourth house. This also encourages you to turn your attention in the direction of home and family, something Libra is inclined to do quite a lot in any case. If standard responses to potentially tricky situations don't seem to work, you need to be original.

28 MONDAY ☿ *Moon Age Day 3   Moon Sign Capricorn*

With so much forward-looking optimism available, today ought to be something of a dream. There is no doubting your sociable qualities while the Sun is in its current position, and you can show how entertaining you can be in any social setting. You could be finding new ways to help those who are less well off.

29 TUESDAY ☿ *Moon Age Day 4   Moon Sign Capricorn*

This is not the best time to adopt a sense of superiority or for feeling that you know better than everyone else. If you do adopt such an attitude, be prepared for the possibility of coming well unstuck! Simply maintaining your usual Libran outlook on life can assist you to draw in admirers. One or two of them might be really attracted to you.

30 WEDNESDAY ☿ *Moon Age Day 5   Moon Sign Aquarius*

This has potential to be a favourable time on the communication front because you also have Mercury in your solar third house right now. If there is something you want, there has never been a better time to ask for it than this. Confrontations of any sort are best avoided today. Discussions are fine, but don't let them get out of hand.

December 2011

1 THURSDAY ☿ *Moon Age Day 6   Moon Sign Aquarius*

Your love life is now positively highlighted and this could be the best time of the month for close attachments. You can also enjoy a renaissance in any creative pursuit, and everything you do looks both beautiful and wise. If you demonstrate how fair and open you can be, don't be surprised if people seek your advice.

2 FRIDAY ☿ *Moon Age Day 7   Moon Sign Pisces*

Daily encounters should benefit you once again, at a time when getting together with other people is more profitable than ever. This is the way you work best, constantly networking and interacting. From a chat over the garden fence to a high-powered brainstorming meeting, it's time to show everyone just what you are made of.

3 SATURDAY ☿ *Moon Age Day 8   Moon Sign Pisces*

As you become ever more resourceful, so you start to realise that December could well be the month during which you succeed beyond your previous expectations. A little self-belief is critical to Libra, and it's time to make full use of it right now. Your creative potential remains highlighted, and you have what it takes to make things beautiful.

4 SUNDAY ☿ *Moon Age Day 9   Moon Sign Pisces*

Ahead of the lunar low it pays to tie up as many loose ends as possible. It's a question of getting to grips with important issues later in the day and not allowing problems to mount up in personal attachments. The more you are willing to listen carefully, but also say what you really think, the greater is the chance that you can make progress.

5 MONDAY ☿ *Moon Age Day 10   Moon Sign Aries*

This week begins with the lunar low but it's probably good to get it out of the way so early in the month. You might not be feeling like pushing over any buses, but that won't necessarily prevent you from having a generally good day. Keep your expectations moderate and your desires to a minimum and all should be well.

6 TUESDAY ☿ *Moon Age Day 11   Moon Sign Aries*

Once again your confidence may not be at its highest, and you might be feeling that things generally are not going quite the way you would wish. As long as you don't react too strongly to minor mishaps you can keep going more or less as you choose. If you find colleagues difficult, bear in mind that they might think the same about you!

7 WEDNESDAY ☿ *Moon Age Day 12   Moon Sign Taurus*

It should now be much easier to express your emotions. This is an ideal time to clear the air and to say things that have been on your mind for quite a while. As December settles in and the winter weather makes itself known, there is much to be said for seeking out a warm fireside and the company of family members.

8 THURSDAY ☿ *Moon Age Day 13   Moon Sign Taurus*

The emphasis is still on enjoying the comforts of home and the security that comes from family ties, but today it has less to do with the weather and more to do with the position of Venus in your solar chart. Be prepared to find ways of putting something right that went wrong in a relationship, maybe months or even years ago.

9 FRIDAY ☿ *Moon Age Day 14   Moon Sign Taurus*

This can be a period of improved relationships and communication with friends. For the first time this week you can happily sally forth and look for new situations and different sorts of mental stimulation. A more expansive attitude works best, and helps you to wake up to some exciting new possibilities that are tied to the season.

10 SATURDAY ☿ *Moon Age Day 15 Moon Sign Gemini*

This is a phase that could be marked by a distinct lack of discipline in practical affairs. In some ways you prefer to let things ride, rather than pitching in and sorting them out once and for all. Ask yourself whether your attitudes are slightly unrealistic, and be willing to talk to someone who has more age or experience than you do.

11 SUNDAY ☿ *Moon Age Day 16 Moon Sign Gemini*

You now have scope to develop your personal identity and your own ideas more than was the case earlier in the week. With everything to play for in the romantic and social stakes, it's time to show how lively and alert you can be. Make the most of events that are happening in your locality, and of the chance to show your gregarious side.

12 MONDAY ☿ *Moon Age Day 17 Moon Sign Cancer*

Your domestic affairs undergo a more expansive phase at this time. Perhaps you are choosing to make changes ahead of Christmas, or simply desire a new way of living your life. The changes don't have to be radical, but they do count, and should help you to feel better about the time of year and more content with your lot.

13 TUESDAY ☿ *Moon Age Day 18 Moon Sign Cancer*

There is a stronger motivation now to work hard and to attain some of the goals that you might have been ignoring of late. Creative potential is especially well marked around now, making this an ideal time to sort out your Christmas decorations. Your ability to entertain others, especially young ones, is under the spotlight at this time.

14 WEDNESDAY ☿ *Moon Age Day 19 Moon Sign Leo*

Dealings with some other people might seem fairly unsatisfactory, particularly if you can't get them to do exactly what you would wish. Present trends also herald a good deal of uncertainty in your mind, together with a tendency to do things time and again, even though you know in your heart they were fine before.

15 THURSDAY *Moon Age Day 20   Moon Sign Leo*

Getting more involved with your friends would be no bad thing now. Social functions are favoured, and the run-up to Christmas has certainly begun. It pays to be quite specific in your wishes and your requests – it's the best way of getting what you want from others. Be prepared to seek out someone you don't see very often.

16 FRIDAY *Moon Age Day 21   Moon Sign Leo*

You have every reason to feel quite optimistic now that the Moon is in your solar third house, and you should also be showing how communicative you can be. Stand by for a few surprises and don't be too alarmed if these make demands on you at short notice. You are equal to any task you set yourself, even if you sometimes doubt it.

17 SATURDAY *Moon Age Day 22   Moon Sign Virgo*

Activities today tend to be more fun than serious, and any truly honest assessment of your life at this time should show you to be generally contented with your lot. Of course there are always things you want that you don't have, but you can achieve some of these in good time. Beware of getting too tied to pointless routines today.

18 SUNDAY *Moon Age Day 23   Moon Sign Virgo*

It appears that personal and intimate matters have potential to bring out the best in you at this time. Concentrating on the family, rather than distant friends or even work, can certainly work wonders. If you find yourself facing a mountain of work, the best approach is to break it down into easily manageable units and do them one at a time.

19 MONDAY *Moon Age Day 24   Moon Sign Libra*

Now you can capitalise on a two-day period with the Moon in your own zodiac sign, and it is towards home and family that you are encouraged to turn your attention. Maybe you are dealing with details associated with Christmas, or perhaps simply reorganising things at home. Whatever you are doing, enjoy the lunar high to the full.

20 TUESDAY
Moon Age Day 25   Moon Sign Libra

Keep your ears open because what you learn in group situations today could prove to be extremely useful in the end. Listen to what is being said and don't commit yourself to joining in unless you are very sure of your ground. Take advantage of the energy that is available today, but beware of taking on more than is probably good for you.

21 WEDNESDAY
Moon Age Day 26   Moon Sign Scorpio

This would be a very good time to benefit from the diversity of interests that is so typical of your Libran nature. With more energy at your disposal and the chance to put it to good use, you have scope to tackle all manner of new jobs. Be prepared to offer help and advice to other people if they request it.

22 THURSDAY
Moon Age Day 27   Moon Sign Scorpio

Some slight caution would be no bad thing, and it's worth realising that there are certain limitations placed upon you at the present time. This may not go down well, particularly if you are feeling a great sense of urgency today. Try to go with the flow in social matters and listen specifically to what family members are saying.

23 FRIDAY
Moon Age Day 28   Moon Sign Sagittarius

Today is a question of taking things steadily and not overestimating your capacity for work. Although there is plenty of energy on offer in general, this may not specifically be the case today. Why not pace yourself and allow others to take some of the strain? If you go to bed tonight feeling drained, you may still feel like that tomorrow.

24 SATURDAY
Moon Age Day 29   Moon Sign Sagittarius

Today could find you on top form and eager for almost anything that comes along. It's possible that you won't feel too much like working, but the holiday season is beginning and Libran people simply love to have fun. Trends indicate a general element of nostalgia, and you are no exception. That's Libra!

25 SUNDAY   *Moon Age Day 0   Moon Sign Capricorn*

It might be better to defer to the ideas of others, rather than causing waves on Christmas Day. You can't expect everything to go according to plan, but when it matters most you should be able to pull out all the stops to give everyone a good time. This is the nature of Libra, because the well being of others is more important than your own.

26 MONDAY   *Moon Age Day 1   Moon Sign Capricorn*

Favourable trends attend Boxing Day, and there's an emphasis on encounters with a number of different individuals today, some of whom might possess information that is both timely and useful. Where love and romance are concerned, it shouldn't be difficult to find the right words to sweep someone off their feet during the festivities.

27 TUESDAY   *Moon Age Day 2   Moon Sign Aquarius*

Maybe you feel slightly restricted, because you need to mix with as many different sorts of people today as proves to be possible. Your strength lies in your ability to come up with a number of different ideas, some of which involve innovation. Seek out individuals who will listen to what you have to say and who may even help.

28 WEDNESDAY   *Moon Age Day 3   Moon Sign Aquarius*

The positive times continue and all aspects of communication are once again stimulated by the presence of little Mercury, which is well placed for you. Specifically, this gives you everything you need to find exactly the right words to say. At a personal level, your chat-up lines are spectacular, and this continues until the New Year!

29 THURSDAY   *Moon Age Day 4   Moon Sign Pisces*

This continues to be a very positive time when it comes to pleasing family members and friends alike. All the same, you can afford to make this 'your' day during the Christmas break, and a time when you can choose to do more or less what suits you. This might include spending at least some time alone. Now there's a novelty!

30 FRIDAY   *Moon Age Day 5   Moon Sign Pisces*

There's no doubt about it – you can come up with plenty of new ideas today, even if actually putting them into practice isn't too easy, what with the holiday period and the necessities of the season. Nevertheless, there is nothing to prevent you from looking at future strategies, and playing one or two of them through in your mind.

31 SATURDAY   *Moon Age Day 6   Moon Sign Pisces*

It pays to treat the last day of the year with a little extra seriousness, though not for long. It's a case of working out what you have and have not achieved across the last twelve months, and also planning ahead. But most of what today should be about is enjoying yourself and making things great for everyone around you, as usual.

LIBRA:
2012 DIARY PAGES

LIBRA:
YOUR YEAR IN BRIEF

Keep up your early efforts during January and February to make something of yourself this year. No effort is wasted in your desire to get ahead and that very pleasant nature of yours can be turned to your advantage in all sorts of ways. You should find benefits from the past re-visiting you now. This is a good time to make up your mind about potential changes within your home.

The months of March and April have much to offer in a personal sense and also show just how practical you can be when you turn your mind to it. All sorts of things get done at home and the fact that the early spring weather may be chilly should barely bother you at all. As March grows older you begin to move about more in the wider world. From the middle of March onwards you also become significantly more assertive.

May and June bring the early summer and should both be months of significant movement and activity. There are gains to be made in matters of love, with new relationships cropping up for some Librans and plenty of chance to show just what a social animal you are. June, in particular, could bring some pleasant surprises when it comes to making more money and for some, a new job is on the cards.

Your life moves on apace during July and August. These are months of great movement and activity. Not only are you likely to be travelling more than has been the case earlier in the year, you are doing so to increase your enjoyment of life. New people come and go but old friends will count the most. For some Librans a new love could be on the cards during August and you will make the most of this in a number of different ways.

Look out for the very real benefits that September and October have to offer. Although in some ways you may feel you are being forced to do things you don't really want to do, there are great potential benefits as a result. Money is easier to come by, though it may fly out of the door very quickly unless you are careful. Keep a sense of proportion regarding new issues, both at work and at home.

The last two months of the year, November and December, should find you anxious to please, slightly slower in your general approach and not so inclined to be moving about all the time. You will have moments to think and to plan, which can prove to be a positive boon later on. Christmas should be particularly inspiring and you can look forward to a time of great happiness for you.

January
2012

1 SUNDAY
Moon Age Day 7   Moon Sign Aries

As the year begins, you could come up against one or two drawbacks, particularly in a social sense. These are due to the placement of the Moon in your opposite zodiac sign, bringing the period known as the lunar low. You won't be on top form today or tomorrow and may decide that a quiet time all round would be best.

2 MONDAY
Moon Age Day 8   Moon Sign Aries

It is time to steady up and to keep your expectations to a minimum. It isn't that you fail to make progress, merely that you are slowed down for today. It is early in the year after all and nobody says you have to keep going at breakneck speed all the time. Spend a few hours in the company of those who love you.

3 TUESDAY
Moon Age Day 9   Moon Sign Taurus

Things improve now. You are likely to be at your best in any sort of group situation, especially if you are the one standing at the front and doing the talking. There is plenty of opportunity to do yourself a great deal of good. There are some financial gains in the offing, probably related to decisions at the end of last year.

4 WEDNESDAY
Moon Age Day 10   Moon Sign Taurus

Contradictions are possible today, particularly in terms of the way people are behaving at work, though you should be quite glad to be back in harness and won't have too much difficulty getting on with people. Gradually you will feel more like your usual self so concentrate on managing to get a good deal done today.

5 THURSDAY
Moon Age Day 11   Moon Sign Taurus

You should be looking at improvements you can make to your life and altering anything that's not right. A long-term plan may be coming to fruition, probably sooner than you thought. The Sun is well aspected in your chart, offering wider horizons and the scent of excitement and change, perhaps giving you an overwhelming desire to travel.

6 FRIDAY
Moon Age Day 12   Moon Sign Gemini

Today would be a good day to come to terms with people who may have given you some problems in the past. You are likely to feel some restlessness today. This is nothing new and the position of the Sun in your chart, though positive in many ways, can be considered the culprit.

7 SATURDAY
Moon Age Day 13   Moon Sign Gemini

You need a weekend that typifies Libra working at its best, which also means variety and excitement. If family pressures make some of this difficult, compartmentalise your life to counter the sense of responsibility. Try to keep life as varied as possible and don't allow yourself to get stuck in any sort of rut.

8 SUNDAY
Moon Age Day 14   Moon Sign Cancer

Someone is likely to seek to offer you some timely advice and it would be at least sensible to listen, even if you decide to follow your own path in any case. All in all, this should be a positive day. Encounters with new people who come into your life could prove to be something of an inspiration now.

9 MONDAY
Moon Age Day 15   Moon Sign Cancer

Your day is likely to be polarised because the working Libran everyone sees right now is so radically different from the person you are when enjoying yourself. Present aspects to the Sun are supporting you in your struggle to make necessary changes, not least of all those associated with your working life.

10 TUESDAY *Moon Age Day 16   Moon Sign Cancer*

Chances are that when it comes to organising your home life, you are extremely co-operative and anxious to show just how giving you can be. This is in stark contrast to the more practical qualities you possess. However, there could be a few people around who find this duality difficult to understand; try not to offend them.

11 WEDNESDAY *Moon Age Day 17   Moon Sign Leo*

This is not a time to panic about anything and you can do yourself a great deal of good by simply playing it cool. If it is fame or even notoriety you are after, this could be just the time you are looking for to push for it. Keep a sense of proportion regarding situations that seem to be running out of control.

12 THURSDAY *Moon Age Day 18   Moon Sign Leo*

It is possible that you are somehow out of your depth or unable to break through the entrenched ideas that others are displaying today. There are some unusual situations to deal with just at the moment and you may feel that your mind is somewhat more muddled than has been the case of late. Be reassured that this is a very temporary state of affairs.

13 FRIDAY *Moon Age Day 19   Moon Sign Virgo*

Things generally are looking good. Today you will feel most happy if you take the chance to stand fairly and squarely in the limelight. The only thing to be sure of is that you understand fully what is being expected of you. If you are not sure of this, make certain you get on top of the situation before you are put to the test in a very public way.

14 SATURDAY *Moon Age Day 20   Moon Sign Virgo*

It's a well-known fact that Libra, like all the Air signs, tends to run pretty much on its nerves. You may give the impression of being bomb proof but nothing could be further from the truth. However, even in situations that have you quaking in your shoes, you manage to put on a very confident face. You may have doubts about your abilities today, but you should feel more confident tomorrow.

15 SUNDAY   *Moon Age Day 21   Moon Sign Libra*

You feel joyful, are easy to talk to and have everyone's best interests at heart, so enjoy the day – even if it turns out to be exhausting. This is not a time to sit and think about things. Set targets for your present restless and searching spirit, and use the potential of the lunar high to make sure this is a day filled with possibilities.

16 MONDAY   *Moon Age Day 22   Moon Sign Libra*

Things are still quite clearly going your way and you should find yourself in a position to influence situations much more than has been the case previously. What matters the most is that you concentrate on making a good impression on others, which should not be difficult. A zippy and carefree nature is quite evident to everyone.

17 TUESDAY   *Moon Age Day 23   Moon Sign Scorpio*

Activity of any sort is right up your street. Most Librans are definitely firing on all cylinders but don't run away with the idea that you can push yourself as hard as you wish. After the lunar high, it is clear you need rest, like everyone else, though there is some doubt as to whether you are getting enough at the moment.

18 WEDNESDAY   *Moon Age Day 24   Moon Sign Scorpio*

You can be sure of support, particularly from colleagues and friends, so keep this in mind when you are making decisions. This would be a great time for Librans who have been looking for love to cast their nets in a different and perhaps even a surprising direction. Explore a new possibility especially one that means some sort of business partnership.

19 THURSDAY   *Moon Age Day 25   Moon Sign Sagittarius*

Such is your popularity that people should gang together to help you at the moment and so this is a good time to get things done. Your capacity for keeping going is good but today might have less sparkle in the social and romantic departments. Start new projects, especially those associated with house and home, as you mean to go on.

20 FRIDAY   *Moon Age Day 26   Moon Sign Sagittarius*

It looks as though you would be best to concentrate on quieter activities today. Your concentration levels should be good and you won't be concerned about working on your own. In fact, watch out that you are not so reserved that others think you are sulking. This is a very short interlude and is not likely to endure much beyond today.

21 SATURDAY   *Moon Age Day 27   Moon Sign Capricorn*

It isn't out of the question that you will have romance on your mind this weekend. If you are a young or young-at-heart Libran, with no attachments, this is the time to keep your eyes open. The more settled amongst you could almost certainly get new rewards from existing ties. Listen to family members who might have interesting things to say.

22 SUNDAY   *Moon Age Day 28   Moon Sign Capricorn*

Libra starts to sizzle again. You need change and diversity, and that added zing you are feeling at present can be pushed in a number of different directions. What others have to say about you now is how good you are to have around. Routines should be thrown out of the window today, as you focus on variety and fun.

23 MONDAY   *Moon Age Day 0   Moon Sign Capricorn*

Good luck could bring some financial gains, so perhaps it's the week to take a small risk. Keep up your efforts to get ahead, and don't be put off by the sort of people who love to bring others down. Irrespective of circumstance, you tend to go around today with a smile on your face and a very definite spring in your step.

24 TUESDAY   *Moon Age Day 1   Moon Sign Aquarius*

Being a Libran, you have the right sort of personality to get on with just about anyone, even though you don't always show how cheerful you really are. Today is a good day to appear confident, even though you may be shaking inside. Family gatherings, in particular, will be a great place to be as you'll be a wonderful person to have around.

25 WEDNESDAY   *Moon Age Day 2   Moon Sign Aquarius*

Today you are very conscientious and when it really matters, you deliver everything that is required of you, and a good deal more besides. Be bold and determined, especially when you are in company that really counts. You won't want certain other people to know when you are unsure of yourself, but you shouldn't worry.

26 THURSDAY   *Moon Age Day 3   Moon Sign Pisces*

Nostalgia is a natural part of today, but you must not allow it to rule the present or influence you for the future. Librans who are looking for a new job should keep their eyes open now. Look out for something from the past catching up with you in one way or another, even if it is just in the way you are thinking.

27 FRIDAY   *Moon Age Day 4   Moon Sign Pisces*

You do need to exhibit a little care today, not only on your own behalf but for the sake of family members and friends too. Taking responsibility for others comes fairly easy to Libra at this time. Avoid minor mishaps at home by taking special care not to do anything you know to be silly or dangerous.

28 SATURDAY   *Moon Age Day 5   Moon Sign Aries*

Along comes the lunar low, which threatens to stop you in your tracks, at least in some respects. You would be best to view today as an opportunity to take a rest. It's true that you won't get as much done as you might wish but there is nothing at all to prevent you from planning strategies for later in the month.

29 SUNDAY   *Moon Age Day 6   Moon Sign Aries*

A planetary lull is in operation, and there really isn't very much you can do about this situation. You could decide to take a rest, of course, which would certainly do you a great deal of good. However, this is not a mood that is very much to your liking and so a degree of patience is called for today while you ride out this influence.

30 MONDAY   *Moon Age Day 7   Moon Sign Aries*

Keep ahead of the crowd by being your cheerful and chatty Libran best. You should sense that you can turn awkward situations around right now. Romantic offers that come your way should be looked at realistically but seriously too. This should turn out to be a positive time to get involved in new interests of just about any sort.

31 TUESDAY   *Moon Age Day 8   Moon Sign Taurus*

If you feel you are up against it in terms of the things you have to do today, look for some help and support that will be more than welcome during this interlude. Don't expect to get everything your own way at the moment. Present trends do tend to hold you back a little, though certainly not so much that you need to worry about it.

February

2012

1 WEDNESDAY
Moon Age Day 9   Moon Sign Taurus

There are things today that need sorting out in a professional sense, and then far more important issues that have a bearing on your personal life. Try hard to make certain they do not become confused. If there is any sort of polarisation going on, between home and work, you will need to divide up your time more carefully.

2 THURSDAY
Moon Age Day 10   Moon Sign Gemini

Don't allow yourself to be tied down to routines too much or you will get bored, which is the last thing you need at present. New input from people who have recently come on the scene could prove interesting. Although there are obligations taking up your time today, you need to make room to move and to feel free.

3 FRIDAY
Moon Age Day 11   Moon Sign Gemini

Although you have plenty on your plate at the moment, this could be a good day to spend some time with family members – there are people around who really need your support at present. Information coming your way may prove to be quite misleading, which is why you need to check and re-check things yourself.

4 SATURDAY
Moon Age Day 12   Moon Sign Gemini

You might have to put in that extra bit of effort today, but the results will be worth it. All affairs of the heart are highlighted and made that much better under prevailing astrological trends. Weigh your options carefully today, but once you have made up your mind about any potential course of action, go for it in a big way.

5 SUNDAY
Moon Age Day 13   Moon Sign Cancer

It is likely that others could be touchy and you will need to be extremely careful about the way you approach them. This is a potentially hard-working time but you will reap the rewards of your efforts in the longer-term. Love life and personal relationships are demanding, indicating a very definite see-saw period at this time.

6 MONDAY
Moon Age Day 14   Moon Sign Cancer

The freedom-loving qualities of Libra are prominent today, so you should try to make sure you are on the move. Even if you only manage a shopping trip, it would be better than nothing. A talk with a friend or someone whose opinions you value could turn out to be extremely useful today, so pay attention.

7 TUESDAY
Moon Age Day 15   Moon Sign Leo

If you take the chance to do a number of very good turns for the people you care about today, it could turn out that you feather your own nest at the same time. Remember that getting all your own way with others today really is not the issue. What is more to the point is making certain you are fulfilling your obligations to those you care for and to yourself.

8 WEDNESDAY
Moon Age Day 16   Moon Sign Leo

It is now important, especially in personal attachments, to talk things through fully and to genuinely listen to what others have to say. It won't be easy, but the results prove to be more than worthwhile. Although you are kind and understanding at present, try to ensure that others don't mistake your motives and misread the situation.

9 THURSDAY
Moon Age Day 17   Moon Sign Virgo

Use your intuition, which won't let you down. If you know instinctively that someone is worthy of your trust, then this is likely to be the case. This would be a good day to do some shopping. You might be looking to people you don't know very well today and find yourself relying heavily on them.

10 FRIDAY
Moon Age Day 18   Moon Sign Virgo

You may have to reorder your schedules somewhat today in order to leave time for possibilities that are only now coming into your mind. Most of the time you will be reacting to what is going on around you. You could find that people are simply not reliable now, which is why you may need to do most things for yourself.

11 SATURDAY
Moon Age Day 19   Moon Sign Libra

You ought to be able to get your own way quite easily now. The lunar high offers better potential than any time so far this month. This is a time when you need to be in a position to shine in a public sense. No matter how much you have to reorganise things, this is the time to get out there and impress people.

12 SUNDAY
Moon Age Day 20   Moon Sign Libra

With a smooth and easy view of life generally, it looks as though you can make some significant gains, without having to try too hard. You are especially tolerant of the way your relatives and friends are behaving at the moment so it's a good thing that you won't take offhand remarks as anything more or over-react to situations.

13 MONDAY
Moon Age Day 21   Moon Sign Scorpio

Look out professionally today. There could be some slight problems with superiors, who have problems of their own and are taking it out on you. Avoid any over-suspicious thoughts at this time. You won't see everything you do as being equally worthy or interesting but routines do have to be addressed at the moment.

14 TUESDAY
Moon Age Day 22   Moon Sign Scorpio

Beware of being argumentative right now, although in general you are more inclined to sulk a little than speak your mind. It is possible that although you know situations could benefit from your input, you simply cannot raise the enthusiasm to get on with them. By tomorrow, this slightly difficult trend will be gone.

YOUR DAILY GUIDE TO FEBRUARY 2012

15 WEDNESDAY   *Moon Age Day 23   Moon Sign Scorpio*

With a fairly neutral day in store, yet plenty of ability to have a bearing on circumstances around you, it would be a good time to show the very inventive side to your nature. If you do, it might not be exactly exciting, but today could prove to be eventful. It's up to your imaginative approach how much you can make happen.

16 THURSDAY   *Moon Age Day 24   Moon Sign Sagittarius*

Those Librans who have been looking for love now find themselves in a particularly good position, so try to move relationships ahead as the object of your desire could well be more willing to respond than of late. You are also handing out plenty of compliments yourself. In a practical sense, look carefully at routine situations and conditions.

17 FRIDAY   *Moon Age Day 25   Moon Sign Sagittarius*

Keep an eye on younger family members, one or two of whom could be experiencing some small problems. A standard response to others probably won't work very well today, which is why you have to adapt to suit prevailing circumstances. Fortunately, that isn't difficult for Libra. People recognise your inherent fairness and tolerance right now.

18 SATURDAY   *Moon Age Day 26   Moon Sign Capricorn*

Variety is certainly the spice of your life over the next couple of days and you will become unsettled if you don't make it happen. Libra is on the move, even if you don't know where you are going yet. You are very reactive today, which is why you shouldn't spend too much time doing only what is expected of you, or you will get bored.

19 SUNDAY   *Moon Age Day 27   Moon Sign Capricorn*

Deeper attachments take something of a back seat, probably because those who are normally closest to you show a tendency to be rather distant now. You need to put yourself in the limelight today, so you can show your real talents, especially in social and professional situations. Some aspects of today are in a sharp contrast to yesterday.

20 MONDAY
Moon Age Day 28   Moon Sign Aquarius

There are some small gains to be made financially, but you will have to keep your eyes open. Don't be shy today. People are watching you and it is important that you give a good impression. This is especially true in a work sense, but you can't rule out the possibility of admirers coming your way too. The end of the day could be somehow special.

21 TUESDAY
Moon Age Day 29   Moon Sign Aquarius

People are now very easily persuaded by your up-front and positive attitude. A little cheek sometimes goes a long way and so you shouldn't be backward about pushing your luck. Keep on moving forward and if there is anything you really want from life, this is almost certainly the best time of the month to go and get it.

22 WEDNESDAY
Moon Age Day 0   Moon Sign Pisces

You should find it easier to get on side with family members but it is in the sphere of romance that the real benefits make themselves known. Kind words are important, either received or spoken. Your mind is very inventive today, so take the opportunity to work on innovative ideas that could be followed up later.

23 THURSDAY
Moon Age Day 1   Moon Sign Pisces

Don't allow yourself to become bored or to be tied down so much with things you simply 'have' to do, that you fail to create the necessary space for innovation and spontaneous action. There are many different ways to do the same job and today would be a fine day to try out some alternatives.

24 FRIDAY
Moon Age Day 2   Moon Sign Pisces

There is an ingenious streak to your nature, which shows itself more and more as the days pass. By this afternoon, you have a strong power to influence people so make sure you use it. You won't get everything you think you want today but you should achieve much of what you need.

25 SATURDAY
Moon Age Day 3   Moon Sign Aries

You might feel a little lacklustre today and unless you are prepared, the lunar low could take the wind out of your sails. If, on the other hand, you decide right from the start that it would be sensible to take things easy today, the worst of the potential difficulties can be mitigated altogether.

26 SUNDAY
Moon Age Day 4   Moon Sign Aries

The lunar low tends to make you very pensive and much quieter than you like to be. Libra is a zodiac sign that influences people to be much more complex than they first appear and who don't always react as might be expected. What can be said about today is that you would be foolish to either push yourself too hard or to indulge in speculation.

27 MONDAY
Moon Age Day 5   Moon Sign Taurus

Don't allow others to push you around and at the same time do what you can to protect those you see as being vulnerable. Before you speak, make sure you are in full possession of the facts. It's time to stand up for yourself, especially against people who tend to have a bullying attitude to life. You seem to be in a reforming state of mind.

28 TUESDAY
Moon Age Day 6   Moon Sign Taurus

What would really bore you at present is to be stuck in the same place all the time, completing one dull task after another. Leave someone else to sort out the details whilst you find ways to have fun. Meanwhile, at home, family members could be asking you for the sort of advice that is difficult to offer. It might be best to keep your own counsel.

29 WEDNESDAY
Moon Age Day 7   Moon Sign Taurus

What you hate most of all at the moment is being kept in one place. People have interesting stories to tell you today, one or two of which might prove to be extremely informative. Wherever possible, opt for a change of scenery if you can, as this is the best way to benefit from the planetary influences.

March

2012

1 THURSDAY
Moon Age Day 8   Moon Sign Gemini

It is possible that life in general will take on a slightly routine sort of feel. Ring the changes socially and hand out some pleasant compliments to those who are closest to you. Stick to what you know and enjoy the company of those you love. With just a few sensible precautions, the slightly negative trends won't have much of a bearing on your day.

2 FRIDAY
Moon Age Day 9   Moon Sign Gemini

This is not the sort of day during which you should have to do things more than once. Indeed, with a little concentration, you should be making a great deal of headway. Your powers of attraction are decidedly strong now, allowing for you to make a very good impression all round and especially so on someone you find personally attractive.

3 SATURDAY
Moon Age Day 10   Moon Sign Cancer

Avoid getting on the wrong side of your partner because that would spoil the sort of magic that is sparking off today. One or two friends may be feeding you with information that is slightly suspect, which is why you might be having some nagging doubts. In the main, though, the positive relationship highlights continue unabated.

4 SUNDAY
Moon Age Day 11   Moon Sign Cancer

A change of scene would do you good, with some fresh air and some distance put between yourself and potential rows. The potential for clashes is caused by present aspects to Mars in your solar chart. You may need to stick up for yourself and are unlikely to want to give ground in any issue you are sure about.

5 MONDAY
Moon Age Day 12   Moon Sign Leo

You know just the right things to say in order to get others on your side, and this ensures that meetings go your way. Plus you can look forward to a little more in the way of good luck, at least over the next three or four days. Socially speaking it appears that you will be on a winning streak this week, and today is no exception.

6 TUESDAY
Moon Age Day 13   Moon Sign Leo

You may think you want to get on well with others, but that is most likely only when they are willing to agree with what you have to say. There is very little compromise about at the moment, and it has to be admitted that you are the one who is pushing to get their own way. Avoid unnecessary red tape in all your dealings with authority today.

7 WEDNESDAY
Moon Age Day 14   Moon Sign Leo

You are probably feeling quite confident, although you may find you are restricted from actually achieving what you want. However, you should take every chance to arrange situations to suit your social life and also to find time for your family. There are plenty of light-hearted moments now, so take the chance to display your sense of humour to the world.

8 THURSDAY
Moon Age Day 15   Moon Sign Virgo

Whatever you undertake today is likely to last, although you may find that the things you are working on take ages to finish. This is probably because you are doing everything so thoroughly. You are definitely in the mood to reorganise. This will include your own life and circumstances, together with those of everyone else!

9 FRIDAY
Moon Age Day 16   Moon Sign Virgo

Libra is at its chatty and sometimes nosy best, so you should be managing to achieve a rapport with many different types of people. You seem to be in a mood to push yourself, but just be careful not to push too hard. You should get positive reactions from most of the people you encounter today and might also discover a few secrets you didn't even suspect.

10 SATURDAY   *Moon Age Day 17   Moon Sign Libra*

Make an early start with important plans and, once you have made your mind up to a specific course of action, don't let anything hold you back. The lunar high offers good communication skills, together with a stronger influence over others and the chance to let the world know exactly what you can do. Make the most of it.

11 SUNDAY   *Moon Age Day 18   Moon Sign Libra*

It is time to rely on your hunches because Lady Luck is definitely going to be on your side now. You should stick with your decisions today and show a more decisive face to the world than has been the case for the last few days. Make sure you leave time for simply having fun and don't be too personally demanding.

12 MONDAY   ☿   *Moon Age Day 19   Moon Sign Scorpio*

Don't worry about being a bit selfish today – it's fine to feather your own nest sometimes. Sorting out the wheat from the chaff, you should find out today just who is reliable and who is not. Penetrating and insightful, you will only involve those people in your practical and material life who are likely to be either helpful or amenable.

13 TUESDAY   ☿   *Moon Age Day 20   Moon Sign Scorpio*

You could be looking to increase your financial wherewithal but this is going to be a protracted process. This isn't likely to be the most dynamic start you will experience this week and it would be sensible to proceed cautiously, especially where new incentives at work are concerned.

14 WEDNESDAY ☿ *Moon Age Day 21   Moon Sign Sagittarius*

Librans who have tended to be off colour during the last week or so should now be noticing a definite improvement, with greater energy. Mundane and domestic matters might prove tiresome today, which is precisely why you should not involve yourself with them at all if you can help it.

15 THURSDAY ☿ *Moon Age Day 22* *Moon Sign Sagittarius*

Libra is really alive at present. You'll be looking for stimulation and increasingly thirsty for personal freedom. This is partly a response to the changing seasons but is also because the Sun is now so well aspected by other planets. This also increases your ability to communicate so it's a good time to plan meetings or otherwise get your message across.

16 FRIDAY ☿ *Moon Age Day 23* *Moon Sign Capricorn*

Socially speaking, you should spend at least part of today with someone you really rate. It might appear that everyone is getting ahead faster than you are at first today, though by the middle of the afternoon you are taking a more realistic view of life generally and should be able to enlist plenty of help when you need it.

17 SATURDAY ☿ *Moon Age Day 24* *Moon Sign Capricorn*

Look out for words of love coming your way, together with a vote of confidence from someone who really matters to you. Get as many jobs out of the way early in the day as you can. If you are feeling frustrated that not everything is going your way at work, you can be reasonably sure that the situation is different at home.

18 SUNDAY ☿ *Moon Age Day 25* *Moon Sign Capricorn*

The innovative side of your nature is definitely on display – be careful you don't go too far and turn into something of a gadget freak. Save some time today to whisper exactly the right words of love when they are needed the most. Although a good deal of concentration is needed now, if you apply yourself you should make progress.

19 MONDAY ☿ *Moon Age Day 26* *Moon Sign Aquarius*

Libra is in a good position today. People are quite willing to back you up, even when your ideas are somewhat contentious. Don't do anything to cause jealousy between other people but since you identify strongly with the aims and intentions of the group, the trends surrounding you today should suit you down to the ground.

20 TUESDAY ☿ *Moon Age Day 27   Moon Sign Aquarius*

A slower pace is likely. There are routines to address early in the day, but later you will be well advised to make personal contact with others. If you do, the evening could turn out to be especially enjoyable and quite rewarding. People you don't see very often could be making contact and you could probably expect letters from far away.

21 WEDNESDAY ☿ *Moon Age Day 28   Moon Sign Pisces*

Your intellect could be stretched today, but you should be up to the challenge. Listen out for a scarcely audible cry for assistance – follow your intuition to find its source. Although this may seem to be a rather demanding period it is, nevertheless, potentially very rewarding.

22 THURSDAY ☿ *Moon Age Day 0   Moon Sign Pisces*

It is fairly obvious that nothing is going to be achieved at this time by rushing your fences. On the contrary, the more careful you are, the greater will be the rewards in the end. You want to get out there and show the world what you are made of. But don't be impatient – you would do better to let matters settle at their own pace.

23 FRIDAY ☿ *Moon Age Day 1   Moon Sign Aries*

If you feel that today is something of an uphill struggle, it may be because you have let a situation become unnecessarily complicated. If it is at all possible to leave responsibilities and efforts until a later date, so much the better. Not everything turns out exactly as you might wish, though if you are not sailing against the wind you may hardly notice.

24 SATURDAY ☿ *Moon Age Day 2   Moon Sign Aries*

You could well be missing your usual energy – the inventive and quick quality that sets your zodiac sign apart. Use this period as a time for recharging your batteries and don't expect to move any mountains. If you insist on pushing against planetary trends, you are merely going to exhaust yourself without any sensible reason.

25 SUNDAY ☿ *Moon Age Day 3* *Moon Sign Taurus*

Stay in the forefront of any activities you are involved in, be honest and don't try to keep back the truth – you are unlikely to succeed and trying will not endear you to others. If you are at work, take pains to reassure doubters and, in doing so, you might even manage to quell a few doubts you have about yourself.

26 MONDAY ☿ *Moon Age Day 4* *Moon Sign Taurus*

If there is a problem today it is that no matter how much you do, there is always something else waiting in the wings. Energetic as you are, you will have to call a halt eventually. All the same, your capacity for work is extremely high at the moment and you shouldn't have any difficulty doing several jobs at the same time.

27 TUESDAY ☿ *Moon Age Day 5* *Moon Sign Taurus*

Moves to alter situations at work might meet some resistance at first but you should hold fast to your chosen course of action. Stay diplomatic when possible. The practical side of your nature is clearly on display today and it appears you can get plenty done out there in the real world.

28 WEDNESDAY ☿ *Moon Age Day 6* *Moon Sign Gemini*

Today offers significant opportunities. Romance shines out and you should seek it out at some stage today. This is especially true in the case of younger Librans or those who are looking for love. Listen carefully to what is being said in your vicinity because even the most offhand comment can have far-reaching implications.

29 THURSDAY ☿ *Moon Age Day 7* *Moon Sign Gemini*

Especially in practical situations, don't be too quick to jump to conclusions but allow situations to mature, especially in a family sense. Enjoy the serene nature of your personal life and show someone how much you care about them. Slowly but surely as the day gets going, you will find your energy levels are definitely on the increase.

30 FRIDAY ☿ *Moon Age Day 8 Moon Sign Cancer*

Be sure to leave some time free to spend with someone who thinks you are the most wonderful person around. Part of your mind goes forward, whilst another bit of it travels into the past. Actually, that isn't such a bad thing because you have a good deal to learn at the moment from the way you dealt with situations previously.

31 SATURDAY ☿ *Moon Age Day 9 Moon Sign Cancer*

Today is likely to usher in a slightly quieter period, at least where material matters are concerned. When it comes to casual conversations, it seems you are as bright and chatty as ever. There is a distinct possibility you'll find it a little difficult to take anything too seriously over the next couple of days.

April

2012

1 SUNDAY ☿ *Moon Age Day 10   Moon Sign Cancer*

This is a good day to be thinking about travel and mental pursuits of all kinds and it is clear that the inquisitive side of your nature is on display too. You should discover that family members are being particularly supportive so enlist their help when you need it. There is a great opportunity today to broaden your horizons in some way.

2 MONDAY ☿ *Moon Age Day 11   Moon Sign Leo*

Libra is not a natural loner and the support that comes from knowing others are on your side is very important. If there is something you have been wanting of late, this might be the very best time to ask for it. Things go better now when you are involved in group activities and when you can call on other people to lend a hand.

3 TUESDAY ☿ *Moon Age Day 12   Moon Sign Leo*

Today you are good to know, inspirational in relationships and warm to your friends. Conversation comes easily to you and allows you to address the worries that a friend finds difficult to express. There is help around if you want it and, even if you don't, it is unlikely that you would let anyone know this.

4 WEDNESDAY ☿ *Moon Age Day 13   Moon Sign Virgo*

Romance is likely to be important today, so make sure you take the opportunity to show your partner, or maybe someone new in your life, just how important you feel them to be. Professional ambitions could receive a definite boost, even if some of your drive and enthusiasm is slightly reduced just now.

5 THURSDAY   *Moon Age Day 14   Moon Sign Virgo*

It would be a very good thing to make an early start today and to deal immediately with ideas that have just come off the drawing board of your busy mind. Later in the day you would be better to relax, a process that won't be at all easy if you are still trying to solve those last little problems. The early bird really does catch the worm today.

6 FRIDAY   *Moon Age Day 15   Moon Sign Libra*

You want to get new projects started and after a couple of days when you were held back, you can feel that burst of energy taking you forward. The lunar high offers you all the incentive and help you could possibly need, together with sufficient vitality to overturn obstacles. Little will stand in your way now so it's full steam ahead for Libra.

7 SATURDAY   *Moon Age Day 16   Moon Sign Libra*

The lunar high continues and there are new openings and opportunities in store right from the very start of the day. You'll soon deal with any little niggles and you should find people generally happy and helpful. The attitude of a colleague can be particularly inspiring so you should push on towards your objectives, helped by that Moon in Libra.

8 SUNDAY   *Moon Age Day 17   Moon Sign Scorpio*

Creative potential is especially good today and you should use your natural ability to make yourself and those around you feel comfortable in your surroundings. Someone you haven't seen for a while could turn up. You are a bit of a charmer today which, though not in the least unusual for Libra, really does show itself more right now.

9 MONDAY   *Moon Age Day 18   Moon Sign Scorpio*

There is a good chance that routines will bore you, so take any opportunity to make life as varied as you can. An instinctive talent for saying the right things really shows itself now. You enjoy particularly good persuasive talents at this time and will be able to talk anyone round, no matter how reluctant they might at first appear to be.

10 TUESDAY *Moon Age Day 19   Moon Sign Sagittarius*

There may be gains coming your way that you didn't expect, though it is certain that you are putting in that extra bit of effort that can make all the difference in the longer term. Keep smiling today because it's clear you have the ability to create a pleasing impression and really should exploit this in a professional sense.

11 WEDNESDAY *Moon Age Day 20   Moon Sign Sagittarius*

Try to keep your responsibilities to the outside world at a minimum, if only because you want to spend more of your time with the ones you love the most. The compliments that come your way now can be very gratifying. This is likely to be a fulfilling time, especially when you are around home and family.

12 THURSDAY *Moon Age Day 21   Moon Sign Capricorn*

A loved one might be doing their best to make you feel more comfortable but no matter how kind their intentions, their actions probably won't suit you at all. With a renewed focus on the domestic scene, you could be trying to sort things out at home that have either annoyed or frustrated you for quite some time.

13 FRIDAY *Moon Age Day 22   Moon Sign Capricorn*

Be certain that others really do want to help you as much as appears to be the case and take advantage of every opportunity to become better known to people who could be influential. You should be in a very jolly frame of mind today and will be anxious to make a good impression whatever you are doing.

14 SATURDAY *Moon Age Day 23   Moon Sign Aquarius*

You should make sure you have a date for tonight as this is an excellent day in terms of personal attachments, and especially romantic encounters that could leave you with a tremendous sense of happiness. As a further bonus, there isn't any doubt that you are quick off the mark today, both physically and mentally.

15 SUNDAY *Moon Age Day 24   Moon Sign Aquarius*

The positive qualities you have enjoyed for most of this month are still present and it won't be difficult to shine when in company. There are certain ideas that will have to be jettisoned now for the greater good. This is a time to sort out basic issues and to decide how you want to proceed for the next few weeks.

16 MONDAY *Moon Age Day 25   Moon Sign Aquarius*

You will need to rely quite heavily on the help and advice coming from others, though bearing in mind what you have done for them in the past, there is no reason at all why the favour should not be returned. You certainly won't find today quite as dynamic as you may have wished.

17 TUESDAY *Moon Age Day 26   Moon Sign Pisces*

Planetary influences mean that social trends are very good and you should aim to mix with as many different sorts of people as you can at this time. Your everyday world should contain more than a few pleasant surprises today and you should notice that others are doing more or less everything they can to support you.

18 WEDNESDAY *Moon Age Day 27   Moon Sign Pisces*

Stay away from pointless rules and regulations which could otherwise get on your nerves, and don't get involved in any sort of puzzle that begins to occupy you totally. You won't have to try too hard to be in interesting places today because you'll be feeling naturally inquisitive and whichever way you turn, you should find something to fascinate you.

19 THURSDAY *Moon Age Day 28   Moon Sign Aries*

It is possible that the lunar low could bring irritation if you can't do exactly what you want, when you want. However, if you realise that present trends are not geared towards material success, you can put some of your schemes on hold and still have a good day. It's all a matter of looking at priorities and dealing with the important things.

20 FRIDAY
Moon Age Day 29   Moon Sign Aries

Because of the lunar low, you are likely to run out of steam much more readily than has been the case at any time so far this month. You need to be very steady today and to look at all situations one at a time. Routines suit you fine and you may decide to make this a family sort of day, in which others take some of the strain.

21 SATURDAY
Moon Age Day 0   Moon Sign Aries

There is a tendency now to act on impulse but there is nothing especially unusual about this for you under present planetary trends. Things could be generally quieter but don't worry because they will liven up in a day or two. There isn't quite the same sense of joy around now that has been present of late but it is returning rapidly.

22 SUNDAY
Moon Age Day 1   Moon Sign Taurus

Despite the fact that you are likely to be very busy today, you should be able to rely on your ability to get things right. This brings the potential to achieve professional successes. You should be aiming to discover and to implement the moves now which are most likely to feather your nest for the future.

23 MONDAY
Moon Age Day 2   Moon Sign Taurus

Don't stop pushing ahead in some way towards a longed-for objective but do remember that there is going to be plenty of time to finalise some important plans. This may be one of the best days of the month in a personal sense, with romantic possibilities there for the taking, and some potentially exciting meetings to be staged.

24 TUESDAY
Moon Age Day 3   Moon Sign Gemini

Someone who hasn't been a part of your scene for quite some time is likely to make a repeat visit to your life, bringing with them a few quite startling surprises. Freedom appears to be the key to happiness and it is obvious that you want to seek out wide-open spaces and places where you can feel unfettered.

25 WEDNESDAY   *Moon Age Day 4   Moon Sign Gemini*

The Moon strengthens in your solar chart and your best moments will come today if you focus on home and family. Trends show conclusively that you are ready to settle down for a day or two, which is no bad thing because you have been burning the candle at both ends for a while. Fortunately Libra does know when to stop and take a break.

26 THURSDAY   *Moon Age Day 5   Moon Sign Gemini*

The spirit of compromise is strong today, so if you have a particular set of issues to sort out with colleagues, you could hardly pick a better day than this. Things mechanical could prove rather unreliable around now. Friendships and group-related matters offer significant rewards if you choose to get more involved.

27 FRIDAY   *Moon Age Day 6   Moon Sign Cancer*

Pride goes before a fall and you won't help yourself too much if you insist on being right about everything at this time. Today demands a touch of humility in anything you do. Meanwhile, your professional life should be getting better and better, leaving you feeling that you can't put a foot wrong. Be careful; this is something of an illusion.

28 SATURDAY   *Moon Age Day 7   Moon Sign Cancer*

Although not everyone wants to join in the fun, there are a significant number of people around who will do everything they can to be of use to you and who will find you very interesting. Current endeavours should move swiftly towards satisfactory conclusions and today is not without its own form of excitement.

29 SUNDAY   *Moon Age Day 8   Moon Sign Leo*

Most people should be kind to you at the moment, especially acquaintances; and since you have plenty of energy at this time, it looks as though you can enjoy an eventful and even exciting day. However it is also true that what happens in relationships around now could put you under a degree of pressure. Don't be surprised if people behave in strange ways.

30 MONDAY
Moon Age Day 9   Moon Sign Leo

You could feel bombarded with information but it is vital that you take the time to make sense of it all. Friends could be demanding your attention later in the day but that is unlikely to bother you too much. Once again you need to be careful when dealing with mechanical objects, which show a definite tendency to be awkward for you at present.

May

2012

1 TUESDAY
Moon Age Day 10   Moon Sign Virgo

You might find it is easier to concentrate on more casual associations for the time being and to leave major issues of love to sort out on another day. Influences regarding personal relationships could be less favourable at the moment and it would be best not to push matters too hard.

2 WEDNESDAY
Moon Age Day 11   Moon Sign Virgo

Be determined in practical issues and push forward with an idea, even if not everyone agrees with you. Your happiest times at the moment seem to be when you are in groups, where you can find a certain sort of freedom and the level of support that could be lacking in other areas of your life.

3 THURSDAY
Moon Age Day 12   Moon Sign Virgo

Don't be afraid to gamble a little, particularly when you know that the risk of failure is small. Pushing yourself quite hard now, you need to approach situations in a very positive frame of mind, which is really all it takes to ensure success. Your mind is working like lightning, especially where puzzles are concerned.

4 FRIDAY
Moon Age Day 13   Moon Sign Libra

Aggravation seems to be a thing of the past and you have the ability to find exactly the right words to say to make those around you feel wanted and happy, so make sure you use them. Progress in most matters should be smooth and what might prove most important right now is the fact that personal relationships are working out so well.

5 SATURDAY   *Moon Age Day 14*   *Moon Sign Libra*

A degree of success is likely to be staring you in the face, probably as a result of things you did in the past. Being certain of yourself is part of what makes today easy. A very hectic phase is at hand, though one that more or less demands you keep up with all the news and views in your vicinity.

6 SUNDAY   *Moon Age Day 15*   *Moon Sign Scorpio*

There is nothing at all wrong with asking for help when you need it and especially not when those around you are so willing to offer support. You may be able to break down a barrier that has been in place for months or even years. Attracting the kind thoughts and goodwill of others certainly should not be difficult for you now.

7 MONDAY   *Moon Age Day 16*   *Moon Sign Scorpio*

The general advice today is to concentrate on what you can do and not to fret over things you can't. Even a single job done well makes your efforts worthwhile at the moment. This is a stop-start sort of day because some of what you want to do is a breeze, whilst other matters seem to be much more awkward.

8 TUESDAY   *Moon Age Day 17*   *Moon Sign Sagittarius*

This is a good day to do everything you can to try to get on well with particularly awkward types. If you don't succeed, it is possible you are trying too hard and need to acknowledge that there are always going to be people who disagree with you. You'll get better results if you concentrate instead on those with whom you have a natural empathy.

9 WEDNESDAY   *Moon Age Day 18*   *Moon Sign Sagittarius*

You should have already noticed that your instincts are spot on at the moment, and you should make the most of that. Communicate directly with others and you will find mutual understanding. There is great scope for attracting life's little luxuries today, something that doesn't generally cross your mind unless you are feeling insecure.

10 THURSDAY   *Moon Age Day 19   Moon Sign Capricorn*

Don't allow yourself to held back by circumstances that seem to be beyond your control; if you look into them further they could turn out to be easy to address and alter. Try to get on side with someone you haven't cared for in the past. A much more decisive edge to your nature generally is the legacy of present planetary trends.

11 FRIDAY   *Moon Age Day 20   Moon Sign Capricorn*

Libra is always active and always thinking. Whilst there do seem to be plenty of interesting things going on around you, you might miss some if you are too preoccupied with what you are doing. Bear in mind that you can't do everything and understand that a little concentration right now can work wonders.

12 SATURDAY   *Moon Age Day 21   Moon Sign Aquarius*

You should find people to be generally supportive and should be out there socialising because the planets really assist you to have a good time. If not everyone has your best interests at heart you can be sure that the people you care about are looking out for you. Enjoyable trends relating to your home life are more than likely around now.

13 SUNDAY   *Moon Age Day 22   Moon Sign Aquarius*

You will get the best out of present trends if you can avoid working too hard and make some time to have fun. Routines will bore you, so enrol other people and get them to lend you a timely hand. Don't worry if each little task is not fulfilled today because there will be a chance to catch up later on. Romance could come knocking later on in the day.

14 MONDAY   *Moon Age Day 23   Moon Sign Pisces*

Romance is on the way for many and with Venus in such a positive position for you, there's a good chance that you find yourself popular with people you didn't think had any time for you at all. Be prepared to alter arrangements at short notice and watch out for a few oddballs in your vicinity. Take life in your stride today.

15 TUESDAY *Moon Age Day 24   Moon Sign Pisces*

Travel would be good today, and so would taking people by surprise. You could be quite shocked at the way some people are behaving and might be put into the position of covering up for something you don't approve of. You need to vary your routines as much as possible today and should not allow minor upsets to get in your way.

16 WEDNESDAY *Moon Age Day 25   Moon Sign Aries*

Don't take on too many commitments today. The lunar low is around and is almost certain to sap your strength. Concentrate on things you enjoy and, if possible, take a total break from responsibilities. You can't expect everyone to agree with your ideas for today or tomorrow, so be patient.

17 THURSDAY *Moon Age Day 26   Moon Sign Aries*

This is not a good time to start any adventures, unless you are absolutely sure of yourself and all the relevant details. Try to find time to relax, if possible with your partner or loved ones. Whilst social developments look better today, you could have more problems with the practical world as lunar low does have a bearing on your life.

18 FRIDAY *Moon Age Day 27   Moon Sign Aries*

You can expect confusing issues to arise early in the day but don't pay them too much attention – they should soon disappear like the morning mist. If you have been looking for compliments from those you really rate, you should be rewarded. Friends, group projects and community concerns should all be high on your list of priorities.

19 SATURDAY *Moon Age Day 28   Moon Sign Taurus*

Now you will actively want to participate in new projects, even if some of these are not of your own making. Convincing colleagues and even family members that you know what you are talking about isn't easy but will be necessary. Romantic interests are definitely looked after well under present trends and you should show how sexy you can be.

20 SUNDAY
Moon Age Day 0   Moon Sign Taurus

You instinctively know what looks and feels right at the moment and you are also very intuitive at this time. In affairs of the heart, you will have the chance to show yourself to be loyal and kind. Others will be very appreciative of the creative side of your nature, which turns out to be very useful to them.

21 MONDAY
Moon Age Day 1   Moon Sign Gemini

Concentrate on the task at hand whenever possible but also be willing to allow others to lend a hand if you can. Look out for new personalities coming into your life. This won't be the most dynamic day you have ever had and you need to be very sure of yourself before you embark on any new projects.

22 TUESDAY
Moon Age Day 2   Moon Sign Gemini

Even strangers seem to have your best interests at heart and actively want to offer sound help and advice. Not everything you hear today is equally worthy of your attention but you can soon sort the wheat from the chaff. Some welcome support and recognition should be forthcoming if you are open to receive it.

23 WEDNESDAY
Moon Age Day 3   Moon Sign Gemini

The long-term gains coming from your progressive and charming nature now are legion. If ever there was a good period for hogging the limelight, this is it. You need to be sure that people are paying attention before you turn your charisma up to full, but once you do, this can be a day to remember.

24 THURSDAY
Moon Age Day 4   Moon Sign Cancer

The longer you think about situations today, the greater your degree of success is likely to be in the longer term. People you don't see very often could play a part in your social life, whilst romance somehow takes a backseat. Don't be in too much of a hurry to get anything done in a practical sense.

25 FRIDAY
Moon Age Day 5   Moon Sign Cancer

It might be party time for some Librans, and also the lure of the outdoors calls you, so you won't want to confine yourself too much today. Once again, romance could be uppermost in your mind and it would be a good day to prove to someone very special that you are fully committed to them.

26 SATURDAY
Moon Age Day 6   Moon Sign Leo

The influences suggest you should be relaxing over the next couple of days, but you won't be too happy to stay in the same place all the time. Get out and about. Those who are at work could find someone higher up in the chain of command to be of specific use.

27 SUNDAY
Moon Age Day 7   Moon Sign Leo

You should be able to find the information you need to move ahead with your medium-term plans, and also be able to attract the right kind of attention when it matters the most. This is an excellent time for exchanging ideas or for fact-finding of any sort. You should not ignore romance today.

28 MONDAY
Moon Age Day 8   Moon Sign Leo

Although there could be some disputes within the family, you are unlikely to be the person who is starting them and you would do well to stay as far away from controversy as possible. There is plenty of optimism about and this would not be a bad time to take on significant new challenges.

29 TUESDAY
Moon Age Day 9   Moon Sign Virgo

There are some very strange and quite unexpected things happening today but that won't bother you too much. Some surprise probably comes from the behaviour of family and friends, which could take you unawares. When it comes to the positive side of life, you almost certainly won't have to look any further than your very satisfying love life.

30 WEDNESDAY *Moon Age Day 10   Moon Sign Virgo*

Your present association with people coming fresh into your life could be particularly noteworthy and it appears you have a great deal to say for yourself no matter what company you keep. There is a continued lively accent on life generally, even if you may find it hard to get everyone to join in.

31 THURSDAY *Moon Age Day 11   Moon Sign Libra*

Your powers of attraction are strong during the lunar high and this is a time when you can take advantage of the fact that you really do turn heads. Things are likely to work out well for you in all sorts of ways, even if there are some jobs that have to be started from scratch – that's not always a bad thing.

June

2012

1 FRIDAY
Moon Age Day 12   Moon Sign Libra

This is a day for going after what you want, even if there are people around who wish to prevent you from doing so. You know your own mind best and, whilst the lunar high is around, you need to make full use of all new possibilities. At work you should be really showing that you are a force to be reckoned with.

2 SATURDAY
Moon Age Day 13   Moon Sign Scorpio

This would not be a good day to shoot from the hip or to wage war with yourself just because things are not going right. Take some time out to smell the roses. Practical matters can put a strain on your patience at the moment and it is very important to realise that a little patience can go a long way.

3 SUNDAY
Moon Age Day 14   Moon Sign Scorpio

Active and enterprising, your mind is working towards a greater sense of autonomy. Not having to rely on others so much is likely to be quite inspiring. However, some support could come from directions that you probably never expected and could be what you need to bring you close to solving a problem that has been around for quite some time.

4 MONDAY
Moon Age Day 15   Moon Sign Sagittarius

Changing planetary trends mean that romance and personal relationships are boosted enormously and you have the ability to improve your social life to the point that you find yourself in almost constant demand. It might take a few days for your potential to really show itself but it is clear that from the start of today you are keen to get cracking.

5 TUESDAY
Moon Age Day 16   Moon Sign Sagittarius

Keep your mind on the future because it is clear that there is no help coming from the past for Libra right now. The attitude of a friend can be both puzzling and humorous. Romance can keep your spirits high and allow you to experience depths of emotion that might have seemed out of the question last month.

6 WEDNESDAY
Moon Age Day 17   Moon Sign Capricorn

Misunderstandings are certainly possible today and it would be sensible to avoid allowing them to get in the way of general progress. Also avoid disputes by letting people know how you feel and by talking as honestly as you can. Making sure others don't misconstrue what you are saying is particularly important at the moment.

7 THURSDAY
Moon Age Day 18   Moon Sign Capricorn

Look out for potential financial gains and remain patient regarding a long-term project that can only mature when the circumstances are right. In the meantime, find ways to have fun with family and friends. There is plenty to capture your attention today, though at least some of it isn't especially relevant to your life as a whole.

8 FRIDAY
Moon Age Day 19   Moon Sign Aquarius

The stronger side of your Libran personality is on display and you are likely to be feeling quite determined. Not everyone takes kindly to the fact that you are presently quite bossy and some sort of compromise could be required. You may find that hard to do because, in the main, your hunches turn out to be correct.

9 SATURDAY
Moon Age Day 20   Moon Sign Aquarius

You should feel more than contented with your lot today but might be inclined to run out of steam if you do too much. A firmer sense of personal and emotional security is required. Intimate relationships are to the fore and those you love the most are giving you renewed reasons to feel extremely happy.

10 SUNDAY   *Moon Age Day 21   Moon Sign Pisces*

Any sort of mystery is certain to grab your imagination and you will enjoy yourself most today if you are solving puzzles or exercising your curiosity. Family members should prove to be very supportive and will offer you new possibilities to think about at home. Curiosity and your general mental powers are well marked today.

11 MONDAY   *Moon Age Day 22   Moon Sign Pisces*

Family-minded Libra puts in an appearance and you would probably rather be at home than anywhere. The sentimental side of your nature is on display. There is something warm and cosy about today, in direct contrast to the somewhat stark realities of life with which you have been dealing for the last two or three days.

12 TUESDAY   *Moon Age Day 23   Moon Sign Pisces*

Lo and behold, your popularity begins to increase yet again and the impression you can make on others if you try is that much stronger. This might turn out to be a very busy day. Your powers of communication are on the up and you show far less of a tendency to speak out without thinking than is sometimes the case for you.

13 WEDNESDAY   *Moon Age Day 24   Moon Sign Aries*

Keep your material sights low for the next few days because, if you do, the lunar low will hardly touch your life at all this time round. The less you bother yourself with material considerations, the greater is going to be the joy you get from relationships and from having the sort of fun that won't cost you a bean.

14 THURSDAY   *Moon Age Day 25   Moon Sign Aries*

Once again you struggle to get ahead in any concrete way and will need to be circumspect about taking chances or risking any money. The attitude of those around you remains positive and there is nothing to prevent you from looking ahead and planning in a progressive way. There are gains to be made today, but not where you expect.

15 FRIDAY
Moon Age Day 26   Moon Sign Taurus

There is time to think right now but also plenty of time to get out and enjoy yourself. Getting together with pals could be fun, especially ones you don't see very often. Material affairs should prove pleasant and rewarding and this is a great time to build upon recent fresh starts you have made.

16 SATURDAY
Moon Age Day 27   Moon Sign Taurus

If you have been looking forward to a trip soon, it might be good to look at all the details and to make certain you have dealt with every potential issue. Someone could string you along personally. In financial terms, you can probably enjoy better times generally, even if this is partly down to luck rather than good planning.

17 SUNDAY
Moon Age Day 28   Moon Sign Taurus

Libra is not always too careful with money but during this phase you would do well to follow up your good ideas and do some planning. You would be well advised to look at the possibility of making new investments, which could offer some gains. Friends ought to be generally supportive but one or two could be rather demanding.

18 MONDAY
Moon Age Day 29   Moon Sign Gemini

Your intuition is strong and should be your best guide at present. You need to be very aware of those you are willing to trust right now. Friends you have known for a long time are probably fine but there could be one or two people about who do intend to pull the wool over your eyes.

19 TUESDAY
Moon Age Day 0   Moon Sign Gemini

Your winning Libran ways are once again on display and a few of the difficulties you thought you were facing blow away on a fresh breeze of optimism. The great thing about being an air sign is that not much bothers you for long at a time. Financial trends are encouraging and you could manage to get one over on a former adversary.

20 WEDNESDAY   *Moon Age Day 1   Moon Sign Cancer*

Although you might not be making the forward strides you would wish in an everyday sense, you will be able to compensate for this by using your natural charm. Bulldozing your way through any obstacle is really not necessary at this time. Libra can be the life and soul of the party at the moment.

21 THURSDAY   *Moon Age Day 2   Moon Sign Cancer*

You won't be stuck for an answer and this is definitely the best time for putting yourself on display. If there are any limitations on your nature during present trends, these are probably self-created. There are plenty of opportunities to hog the limelight, though you may be tiring of having to smile so much.

22 FRIDAY   *Moon Age Day 3   Moon Sign Cancer*

Don't let opportunities slip by simply because you haven't prepared yourself properly. This would be a good time to consider instigating new business partnerships. Success comes at the moment partly through being well organised. You can fall down only if you haven't thought through all the eventualities.

23 SATURDAY   *Moon Age Day 4   Moon Sign Leo*

A heavily competitive element comes along now, forcing you to look at even existing circumstances in a radically different way. You won't want to lose at any game or sport, whilst in terms of career prospects, your mind is working overtime. All the same, find a few hours to enjoy yourself.

24 SUNDAY   *Moon Age Day 5   Moon Sign Leo*

Practically speaking, this is a time of high achievement. Avoid unnecessary discussions about situations that don't interest you and which you cannot alter. Though your dealings with others in social settings could be somewhat strained, there are those amongst your friends who rate you highly.

111

25 MONDAY
Moon Age Day 6   Moon Sign Virgo

Concentrate on the task at hand and avoid allowing yourself to become diverted by situations that don't really need your special touch at all. It is very important to remain focussed for the remainder of this week. Meanwhile, this is a productive day and one that might easily lead to better recognition of your talents from the world at large.

26 TUESDAY
Moon Age Day 7   Moon Sign Virgo

Conforming to the expectations of certain family members won't be too easy and you may need to show a more tolerant face than you often do, particularly when dealing with younger people. A successful time can be expected in love affairs, whether these are of the lifelong variety or simply temporary assignations.

27 WEDNESDAY
Moon Age Day 8   Moon Sign Libra

Not only are you on top form mentally but you should notice that your physical condition is better than normal. With determination and a genuine desire to help others as well as yourself, you are able to forge completely new paths to personal and social success. Avoid pointless rows along the way.

28 THURSDAY
Moon Age Day 9   Moon Sign Libra

You should be able to accomplish a great deal today. There are strong planetary forces on your side, even apart from the lunar high. Now is the time to identify what you want from life and then to go out and get it. Gathering support for any cause close to your heart should be child's play at present.

29 FRIDAY
Moon Age Day 10   Moon Sign Scorpio

Now you can break through barriers that might have looked high and wide indeed in the recent past. You could be left wondering why you were intimidated in the first place and you will definitely be sharpening your persuasive skills and general intellect today. Your unique personal touch is important with new plans so don't simply follow the herd.

30 SATURDAY
Moon Age Day 11   Moon Sign Scorpio

Stay away from what you see as being pointless rules and regulations because these will only annoy you. Friends should prove to be both supportive and very interesting as the day wears on. Your nature has much strength now and you will not retreat from a challenge. Exciting social encounters can also be expected today.

July

2012

1 SUNDAY
Moon Age Day 12   Moon Sign Sagittarius

Although you have what it takes to get on the right side of most people, there are always going to be exceptions. Expect rules and regulations to get on your nerves around this time. All you can do is to shrug your shoulders and smile. You can expect a few ups and downs today, most likely in terms of relationships.

2 MONDAY
Moon Age Day 13   Moon Sign Sagittarius

There isn't much mileage in staying in the same place, and travel of any sort is supported by a number of present trends. In sporting activities, you will be going for gold, though it has to be said that you might only manage silver. You should be on the move today and happy to have things going your way.

3 TUESDAY
Moon Age Day 14   Moon Sign Capricorn

This would be a good time for visiting places of entertainment of for organising romantic twosomes. In a more practical sense, you should be trying to show that you can be trusted with money, even money belonging to others. Social and romantic developments should see you taking the starring role.

4 WEDNESDAY
Moon Age Day 15   Moon Sign Capricorn

The most casual comment now gives you pause for thought and might lead to something stupendous in the fullness of time. Because you are presently very chatty, yet able to listen carefully too, you can have the best of both worlds. All aspects of communication remain important, even if they don't seem so at the time.

5 THURSDAY
Moon Age Day 16   Moon Sign Capricorn

It might seem as though goals and objectives are a long way from sorting themselves out as you might have hoped and a greater degree of intervention is called for. In other words, you are thinking on your feet. In terms of your career, you should review a particular plan of action that isn't working out quite the way you had intended.

6 FRIDAY
Moon Age Day 17   Moon Sign Aquarius

Contemplative and even somewhat nostalgic today, you won't want to push yourself too hard. Keep an open mind about the way family members and friends are behaving at present and simply smile to yourself. By tomorrow the world is your oyster again and it can also be today, though in a less dynamic way.

7 SATURDAY
Moon Age Day 18   Moon Sign Aquarius

Travel is a possibility, as would be a shopping spree or a simple change of scene in the company of friends. What you need most at the moment is entertainment. Even a small change from the routine sort of day that has been common of late will be enough to keep you happy and entertained.

8 SUNDAY
Moon Age Day 19   Moon Sign Pisces

With almost everyone willing to show you how friendly they can be, you should be taking this opportunity to get your own way. Romantic moments pepper the day so don't miss the chance to use your poetic skills to find just the right words. The best advice today is relax and enjoy yourself.

9 MONDAY
Moon Age Day 20   Moon Sign Pisces

It doesn't matter how hard you work, if you are not being seen to do better than your best, it will do you no good in terms of progress. It's unlikely you will be hiding your light under a bushel today, and a good job too! It helps to know the right people and that is what you are making sure to do at work today.

10 TUESDAY
Moon Age Day 21   Moon Sign Aries

This is a time during which you may actively choose to sit back and take stock of situations, if only because the arrival of the lunar low allows you little chance for moving forward. Prior planning is always a good thing, though it isn't something Librans always take into account enough. You are able to do so now.

11 WEDNESDAY
Moon Age Day 22   Moon Sign Aries

Concerted effort counts later but for now you can afford to be just a little circumspect. You could encounter a few obstacles at the moment so don't be too quick to take the initiative. At the same time, it is important not to be restricted by your limitations, many of which will not be there at all by tomorrow.

12 THURSDAY
Moon Age Day 23   Moon Sign Taurus

Any minor mishaps that occur today are likely to be funny rather than serious especially because your sense of humour is finely tuned at present. Not everyone shows quite the patience that you seem to have right now. Some things can be thrown into disarray, thanks to the present planetary trends surrounding you.

13 FRIDAY
Moon Age Day 24   Moon Sign Taurus

The more calm and collected you remain, the greater the chance you will bring even the most awkward people round to your point of view. Some of those people you come across over the next few days seem to exist to test your patience. The way forward is very clear but difficult to follow – don't rise to the bait.

14 SATURDAY
Moon Age Day 25   Moon Sign Taurus

It isn't hard for you to modify your nature to suit that of the people around you and you show a definite ability to adapt in a moment-by-moment sense. Intellectually speaking, it is clear that you are on top form around this time. When it comes to the social side of life, you are at your very best now and show this all the time.

15 SUNDAY ☿ *Moon Age Day 26* *Moon Sign Gemini*

You may be feeling rather assertive and even argumentative today. The problem is that you know how things should be done and you won't have too much patience with those who refuse to accept your point of view. Try not to let this lead to arguments, which will be counter-productive.

16 MONDAY ☿ *Moon Age Day 27* *Moon Sign Gemini*

You should be quite selective today and stick to those areas of life that are going according to plan. Spending some time with those you love the most can prove comforting, and should support you through a slightly irritating patch. There is no sense in trying too hard to go in directions that clearly are not working.

17 TUESDAY ☿ *Moon Age Day 28* *Moon Sign Gemini*

You need fresh fields and pastures new and won't be happy if you have to stick around the house today. If you have to be in one place, make use of your fertile imagination to find the stimulation you need. If there is one thing that is really likely to make you enthusiastic at the moment, it is the possibility of travel.

18 WEDNESDAY ☿ *Moon Age Day 29* *Moon Sign Cancer*

Although life is not exactly tedious right now, it isn't likely to be especially exciting either. Of course, there's nothing preventing you from putting in that extra bit of effort that could make the difference, so get cracking. All the same, an improvement to the smooth running of plans may be the only thing to set today apart.

19 THURSDAY ☿ *Moon Age Day 0* *Moon Sign Cancer*

Although you can easily manage on your own, it appears that things do work out better when you are willing to take on board the opinions of others. Why not try putting your heads together? The greatest fulfilment in your life right now comes from group involvements of one sort or another.

20 FRIDAY   ☿   *Moon Age Day 1   Moon Sign Leo*

It is now extremely important to monitor the opinions of people who are in the know, particularly in a professional sense. Gains come through seeing all your opportunities clearly. You tend to be attracted to unconventional types today and make it very plain that you are not prepared for a run-of-the-mill sort of day.

21 SATURDAY   ☿   *Moon Age Day 2   Moon Sign Leo*

There is nothing ordinary either about today or your way of looking at it. From the moment you get out of bed it is important to push forward progressively and with single-mindedness. Enthusiasm is the key word, and you are certainly in the right frame of mind now to get more or less what you want from life.

22 SUNDAY   ☿   *Moon Age Day 3   Moon Sign Virgo*

Getting the person you care about the most to feel special is important, particularly if they have been down for some reason. There is a very selfless feel to Libra at present, which others will love. Social events are particularly well highlighted and remain so for the next few days.

23 MONDAY   ☿   *Moon Age Day 4   Moon Sign Virgo*

After a few days that should have been fairly relaxing, you might find it difficult to get going today. Not everyone seems to have your best interests at heart, so use your intuition. Social developments seem to be making good ground, though the real emphasis of the day is towards work matters, even though they might seem a little tedious.

24 TUESDAY   ☿   *Moon Age Day 5   Moon Sign Libra*

The lunar high should bring a very positive and assertive feel to the week as far as you are concerned. Don't allow small matters to hold you back and wherever possible do what you can to get ahead professionally. It's the big picture that matters at the moment and you are very determined today.

25 WEDNESDAY ☿   *Moon Age Day 6   Moon Sign Libra*

You could have more luck on your side than you could ever have imagined and will want to exploit it for all you are worth. The sporting side of Libra is also likely to be on display, making it certain that you are being noticed by almost everyone around you. Finding time for social activities is also important, if somewhat difficult.

26 THURSDAY ☿   *Moon Age Day 7   Moon Sign Libra*

Don't be too quick to jump to negative conclusions because the lunar high is still very supportive in most spheres of your life. What might matter to you most at present is your tremendous popularity. Physical and emotional strengths are at a peak, allowing you to feel good and to act with significant determination.

27 FRIDAY ☿   *Moon Age Day 8   Moon Sign Scorpio*

It would be much better, if you are facing some sort of test in the near future, to revise slowly and steadily. In a more personal sense, try to explain the way you feel before you are asked. Libra is not usually the biggest risk-taker, though you may be drawn into it now. Stop yourself; it isn't necessary and it takes a great deal out of your nerves.

28 SATURDAY ☿   *Moon Age Day 9   Moon Sign Scorpio*

The sheer magnetism of your personality can make you very popular at this time and you should have no difficulty bringing people round to your point of view. As usual, you can be a very convincing talker today and it is unlikely that anyone will question either your knowledge or the way you put it across.

29 SUNDAY ☿ *Moon Age Day 10   Moon Sign Sagittarius*

You should find lots of people are asking for your support and you should be happy to help. Although your patience could easily be tested in some way today, in the main you are moving away from the negative trends brought about by the odd recent planetary reversal and should be able to see the way ahead very clearly.

30 MONDAY   ☿ *Moon Age Day 11*   *Moon Sign Sagittarius*

Comfort and security now seem less important as you encounter the first of a series of astrological trends that make it possible, and even desirable, for you to travel. Social trends are on the up and you should feel a wind of optimism dispelling some of the negative qualities of the last few days.

31 TUESDAY   ☿ *Moon Age Day 12*   *Moon Sign Capricorn*

Avoid arguing about anything today but do be willing to take part in reasonable discussions in which you do as much listening as talking. There could be a few small downsides to life and one of these may be the fact that you find it rather difficult to come to terms with the opinions of your partner.

August 2012

1 WEDNESDAY ☿ *Moon Age Day 13* *Moon Sign Capricorn*

Compliments come thick and fast in the professional arena. You have the personal flair to carry off a few prizes in life at the moment. It's true that you can't presently predict the way others are likely to behave, but in the main you should find those closest to you willing and able to lend a hand.

2 THURSDAY ☿ *Moon Age Day 14* *Moon Sign Aquarius*

Although you might have thought that this would be a good time to be on the move, in the end what hearth and home have to offer could be better. Leave a few jobs until later, or else look around for someone else to do them for you. A period of domestic reward greets you for today at least.

3 FRIDAY ☿ *Moon Age Day 15* *Moon Sign Aquarius*

This is not a good day to be beating about the bush or to be pretending that you feel differently than you do. Truthfulness works out well, but of course there is always a limit, even to how honest you can be. If you suspect that someone is trying to give you the run-around, it would be best to let them know how you feel.

4 SATURDAY ☿ *Moon Age Day 16* *Moon Sign Pisces*

Libran know-how allows you to get away with things that others could only dream about. There is scope for broadening your personal horizons around now and a good deal of excitement is possible under present trends. Although you are inclined to act on impulse at the moment, you can usually get away with less concrete planning than usual.

5 SUNDAY ☿ *Moon Age Day 17   Moon Sign Pisces*

It looks as though you are developing a real taste for the finer things in life, perhaps in part as a result of the generosity of someone else. Opportunities for friendships come along thick and fast around now. Your ability to assert yourself is noteworthy too, bringing a more practical period and allowing you to get your own way.

6 MONDAY ☿ *Moon Age Day 18   Moon Sign Aries*

For the next two days, things are going to slow down and you can't expect to make the level of progress that you have done so far this month. If you get yourself into the right frame of mind, you won't mind too much about taking it easy. If you could do so on a beach or in the country, so much the better.

7 TUESDAY ☿ *Moon Age Day 19   Moon Sign Aries*

A personal plan probably won't work out as you had either expected or hoped, so there are going to be a few disappointments. But since there seems to be very little you can do about this situation, you will just have to be patient because by later on tomorrow things should be looking just as positive as they were a few days ago.

8 WEDNESDAY ☿ *Moon Age Day 20   Moon Sign Aries*

Avoid confusion by making sure to say what you think, even though there are a few people around who probably do not want to listen. There are times today when you need to really pay attention. Venus in its present position is favourable for relationships of all types, but particularly good in terms of love.

9 THURSDAY *Moon Age Day 21   Moon Sign Taurus*

Things improve. Your mental and communicative powers are allied at the moment. This means that the things you say have great clout and that people will certainly listen to you. Any confusion early in the day, particularly regarding personal matters, should soon be sorted out, leaving you feeling fairly mellow.

10 FRIDAY
Moon Age Day 22   Moon Sign Taurus

You need to realise today that all situations are a balance and that it is possible to disagree with other people without falling out. Differences of opinion at home are likely to show themselves today. This only becomes an issue if you refuse to take a sensible point of view and insist on saying that you are right.

11 SATURDAY
Moon Age Day 23   Moon Sign Gemini

Getting out in the fresh air is particularly important during August as a whole, and more or less essential around now. Attracting life's little luxuries ought to be rather easier than usual at present. As a rule you are just too busy to notice such things but right now you do enjoy been cosseted in some way.

12 SUNDAY
Moon Age Day 24   Moon Sign Gemini

Once again, aim to get some time out of doors. All the hard work in the world is only sensible if you know how to enjoy yourself when you are not toiling away. Allow someone else to take the strain. The focus now tends to be upon leisure and your social life, which is not at all surprising at this time of year.

13 MONDAY
Moon Age Day 25   Moon Sign Gemini

You should try to ring the changes today because doing the same things for hours at a stretch does not suit you. Best of all, embark on some sort of journey. A new balance comes along in a domestic sense, making it easier for you to get on side with family members who could have proved difficult in the recent past.

14 TUESDAY
Moon Age Day 26   Moon Sign Cancer

Over the last few weeks, you have developed the opinion that unless you are doing things yourself, they are not being done properly. You could find out today that this is not true. Although you could be rather less enthusiastic than you would wish to be, this fact offers others the chance to have a go.

15 WEDNESDAY   *Moon Age Day 27   Moon Sign Cancer*

In the main, your domestic life should be quite settled but there could be a slight upheaval at some stage today. Try to avoid allowing this to upset your equilibrium and settle for a steady and generally happy day. The urge to travel remains strong at the moment but journeys may have to be slightly delayed.

16 THURSDAY   *Moon Age Day 28   Moon Sign Leo*

There ought to be plenty of good weather to come and you will want to the make the most of it. Something you have worked towards for a long time may now be bearing fruit in a significant way. Attracting the good things in life should be quite easy today. Avoid concerns over issues that you cannot control.

17 FRIDAY   *Moon Age Day 0   Moon Sign Leo*

Love is uppermost in your mind so you should choose this time to show someone special how much you care. Today's influences should have a positive bearing on all aspects of communication. Talks and discussions can work out to your advantage and bring you closer to realising a few ambitions.

18 SATURDAY   *Moon Age Day 1   Moon Sign Leo*

Often, when Librans have money, they tend to spend it. However, this year you could have been putting a little by and that can make all the difference right now. The next couple of days offer the chance of some variety in your domestic life so make the most of it. In the financial sphere, you can expect a little more luck than of late.

19 SUNDAY   *Moon Age Day 2   Moon Sign Virgo*

You have a very astute head on your shoulders and are also in a good position to see a host of different possibilities and strategies around this time. Libra is both confident and comfortable at the moment, and it shows. Financial planning undertaken now is likely to work out well.

20 MONDAY
Moon Age Day 3   Moon Sign Virgo

Don't be inclined to sit on the fence regarding issues you know to be important. Even if it means disagreeing with a friend, you have to speak your mind. Although it is clear you are looking for a high degree of personal freedom right now, you need to get important jobs out of the way before you think about taking a break.

21 TUESDAY
Moon Age Day 4   Moon Sign Libra

There is massive support around if you are willing to go out and look for it, not to mention more than your fair share of talent. Libra shines, and this is something everyone is quite keen to see. Put your impressive personality to the test and show the world what you are capable of doing.

22 WEDNESDAY
Moon Age Day 5   Moon Sign Libra

The lunar high takes you out of yourself and improves your ability to handle several different tasks at the same time. Now you can be the life and soul of any party – including some you are planning yourself. Lady Luck is on your side, though you would still be well advised not to speculate too much.

23 THURSDAY
Moon Age Day 6   Moon Sign Scorpio

You should try to bring your astute nature and strong intuition into play in which case your decisions will be quite considered. You should find routine tasks are quite easy to accomplish but you would probably prefer to indulge your need for change and travel. What matters about today is eliciting the right sort of help for whatever you are planning.

24 FRIDAY
Moon Age Day 7   Moon Sign Scorpio

Your intuitive powers are at their peak, allowing you to weigh up situations almost instantly. With a slight change of emphasis, people now see you as someone who is good at talking, rather than a contentious individual. Joint financial endeavours and co-operative ventures are well accented right now.

25 SATURDAY   *Moon Age Day 8   Moon Sign Sagittarius*

Winning others round to your point of view, even beyond personal attachments, ought to be quite easy. Fortune favours the brave and you have more than a little courage on show for the days that lie ahead. If you had been planning on taking a chance in any romantic sense, now is the time to do it.

26 SUNDAY   *Moon Age Day 9   Moon Sign Sagittarius*

Where others are concerned, you continue to show a gracious and generous face to the world at large. At the same time a feeling of self-fulfilment is almost crucial at present. There is no point in continuing to do anything unless you can be sure that it will match up to your expectations of yourself.

27 MONDAY   *Moon Age Day 10   Moon Sign Capricorn*

If you suddenly realise there is a job you should have done that is still waiting, now is the time to get cracking. Your capacity for work is very good at the moment and you have great staying power. Things are likely to be well on course generally and there is every chance you could find some special moments today.

28 TUESDAY   *Moon Age Day 11   Moon Sign Capricorn*

Give yourself a pat on the back for recent successes but don't allow any situation to stand still. You have a good deal going for you at the moment and it's a fact that other people notice this too. It is now time to take a look at what is really working in your life and to discard anything that is not.

29 WEDNESDAY   *Moon Age Day 12   Moon Sign Aquarius*

When you do have free hours at the moment, you will be happiest if you spend a good proportion of them supporting other people, particularly friends in difficulty. Also, there is a continued accent on work and material considerations, so much so that you might find it difficult to spend any time doing exactly what you want.

30 THURSDAY　　*Moon Age Day 13　Moon Sign Aquarius*

Controlling your desire for new information is going to be difficult, though for now you ought to be concentrating on more or less routine tasks. The time for real change could be a few days off. Look out for setbacks in the workplace and deal with them as soon as possible.

31 FRIDAY　　*Moon Age Day 14　Moon Sign Pisces*

Keep a sense of proportion in relationships and don't get too serious with a relationship you have always known to be basically casual. Also, turn away from any desire to keep up with the Jones's. Today finds Venus in a very good position to help you overcome obstacles at work.

September

2012

1 SATURDAY
Moon Age Day 15   Moon Sign Pisces

Spend some time today with friends who have the ability to make you laugh. Though some matters associated with work are something of a chore right now, you should still be able to get through a good deal of work before real boredom begins to set in. When it does, you need to ring the changes.

2 SUNDAY
Moon Age Day 16   Moon Sign Pisces

You show yourself to be even more considerate and kind now than you usually are. The present position of the Sun in your solar chart is part of the reason, though it is fair to say that your present actions and reactions are fairly typical of kind Libra. Pour some oil on any troubled water you observe in the family.

3 MONDAY
Moon Age Day 17   Moon Sign Aries

This is not the best time to expect to get your own way in everything. Your perspectives are somewhat obscured by the presence of the lunar low. Rather than trying to do too much in a practical or material sense, maybe you should spend at least a part of today doing something that pleases only you.

4 TUESDAY
Moon Age Day 18   Moon Sign Aries

People could very easily be digging in their heels today and it won't do you any good at all to force issues. Getting genuine movement into your life today is a little like trying to push water uphill. Settle for a quiet sort of day and spend your time clearing the decks for action that comes later.

5 WEDNESDAY   *Moon Age Day 19   Moon Sign Taurus*

People out there in the world at large are almost certain to be doing you more than the occasional favour at this time. Call on the support of friends when it comes to possible advances at work and don't worry too much about who you rely on if you need good advice.

6 THURSDAY   *Moon Age Day 20   Moon Sign Taurus*

Once you get the ball rolling today, your partner and perhaps some of your pals should be willing to join in the fun. Finding good company is not difficult around this time and you may see it as essential. However, it would be very easy to become bored, which is why you have to work extra hard to make things happen.

7 FRIDAY   *Moon Age Day 21   Moon Sign Taurus*

Be willing to take a longer-term point of view, though even by tomorrow this will cease to be necessary. There are great times in store so take a deep breath and prepare. Positive situations now come as a result of discussions and life is likely to look good, even if you can't get exactly what you want immediately.

8 SATURDAY   *Moon Age Day 22   Moon Sign Gemini*

Trends suggest that the next couple of days should be offering more adventurous and interesting times than have been possible of late. Meanwhile, you should be able to deal with work matters in no time at all. You might be thinking about new friends, especially since one or two people seem to be singling you out for attention.

9 SUNDAY   *Moon Age Day 23   Moon Sign Gemini*

You might do well to focus as much as possible on finances and the way you can feather your own nest for the future. Advertise your presence whenever it proves to be possible because there is no point in hiding your capabilities now. You should feel a growing confidence, perhaps in unexpected areas.

10 MONDAY
Moon Age Day 24   Moon Sign Cancer

Your intuition is especially strong at the moment and you shouldn't turn away from what it is trying to tell you. You may show a slight susceptibility to specific small ailments, so stay away from people who have colds or flu. It is important to follow your heart when it comes to expanding your horizons right now.

11 TUESDAY
Moon Age Day 25   Moon Sign Cancer

If you find yourself acting on impulse, particularly romantically, simply understand that this is the way Librans sometime behave. People you meet socially or at work are now more than likely to offer you new incentives and reasons to think matters through in ways that you haven't noticed before.

12 WEDNESDAY
Moon Age Day 26   Moon Sign Cancer

There should be time for everything today, even if you have to do some jobs with slightly less professionalism than you would wish. A more caring and sharing sort of Libran becomes obvious to everyone and the result of that will be that those you are closest to will be willing to tell you how they feel.

13 THURSDAY
Moon Age Day 27   Moon Sign Leo

You are particularly sensitive at the moment and perhaps inclined to give in too easily if you are on the receiving end of any hard luck story. Emotional relationships should be the ones that offer the most reward at present, and they will bring you to a better understanding of your innermost feelings.

14 FRIDAY
Moon Age Day 28   Moon Sign Leo

It is unlikely to be you who is in an argumentative frame of mind but rather other family members. Don't allow your home to become a battleground and make certain that you stop rows in their tracks before they have a chance to gain momentum. In a social sense you may prefer to stick with friends rather than relatives today.

15 SATURDAY
Moon Age Day 29   Moon Sign Virgo

It's late in the year for a spring clean but that is more or less what seems to be happening. Don't keep hold of anything simply for the sake of habit. You may have to be slightly ruthless. This might be a good time to look at the way your life is structured and a period for making necessary changes.

16 SUNDAY
Moon Age Day 0   Moon Sign Virgo

Understanding what makes other people tick should be quite easy and you can force real gains as a result. You are very sympathetic at present and would be quite willing to change your own direction in life a little in order to help someone else. If you have any problems today, turn on your intuition and see what it is telling you.

17 MONDAY
Moon Age Day 1   Moon Sign Libra

This should be an excellent time for making fresh starts and for coming to terms with the fact that situations generally are looking up. Materially speaking, you are now likely to be doing rather better than of late. Your general level of good luck is worth putting to the test and this would be a good time for signing contracts or other documents.

18 TUESDAY
Moon Age Day 2   Moon Sign Libra

The joking, mischievous side of your nature is clearly on display, to the amusement of practically everyone. Be definite today and you may get more than you expected. The lunar high extends further into the new week, making certain you will spend at least today looking for as many good times as you can find.

19 WEDNESDAY
Moon Age Day 3   Moon Sign Scorpio

A refreshing change of scene would bring its own rewards and you are now in the middle of yet another period during which a vacation would seem possible. Today's planetary focus looks good for putting you in touch with people, both those you mix with regularly and also people you haven't seen for a while.

20 THURSDAY   *Moon Age Day 4   Moon Sign Scorpio*

You are clearly available for any good time that is in the offing and will contribute heavily to the good times in store. Acquiring cash should be quite easy over the next few days. The spirit of harmony and togetherness that is present at the moment is thanks to some beneficial planetary aspects formed by the Moon.

21 FRIDAY   *Moon Age Day 5   Moon Sign Sagittarius*

In terms of your work life, you may be able to close a circle in some way and it does look as if new starts with alternative responsibilities are coming along for many Librans. This part of the month would make a fine time for pleasure trips and tends to be quite a nostalgic time too.

22 SATURDAY   *Moon Age Day 6   Moon Sign Sagittarius*

Any Libran who has been looking forward to a long journey may not have to wait much longer. There are gains to be made from input from family members, some of whom are coming up with extremely good ideas at present. In addition to possible travel, hopeful news could easily be coming from far-off places.

23 SUNDAY   *Moon Age Day 7   Moon Sign Capricorn*

The more domestic qualities of your nature are beginning to show and you are unlikely to be quite as adventurous right now as has been the case recently. With some slight insecurity, you will be pleased to have the reassurance of loved ones. It may seem that home is the best place to be at present.

24 MONDAY   *Moon Age Day 8   Moon Sign Capricorn*

This is a day to watch closely what is going on and not to allow complications to arise when you could so easily sort them out almost immediately. Leave a little time free today in which to simply enjoy yourself. Don't allow practical situations to run into the buffers simply on account of a lack of attention on your part.

25 TUESDAY   *Moon Age Day 9   Moon Sign Aquarius*

The kind of circumstances in which you find yourself are typical of those that often captivate the Libran mind. Information comes from a number of different directions and the especially enjoyable part, as far as you are concerned, is that they all help you to move forward. Expect the pace of activity to be brisk and enjoyable.

26 WEDNESDAY   *Moon Age Day 10   Moon Sign Aquarius*

You do show a tendency to dominate in romantic situations, though this could not be called a fault and is likely to work out well for you in the end. You are likely to feel enthusiastic and you can combine that with a sense of optimism to turn unlikely circumstances to your advantage.

27 THURSDAY   *Moon Age Day 11   Moon Sign Aquarius*

You need to be a good analyst and to avoid taking anything at face value. You won't be short of confidence, but be cautious because too much of that commodity can be quite destructive. Playing devil's advocate isn't fun but can be necessary. There are a few illusions around today, the problem being that some of them look quite seductive.

28 FRIDAY   *Moon Age Day 12   Moon Sign Pisces*

Don't take on any project in which you are beaten before you start. For this reason alone it might be better to stick with what you know for today and leave innovation until later. You have certain goals and objectives in mind, but this is not the day to go all out to achieve them.

29 SATURDAY   *Moon Age Day 13   Moon Sign Pisces*

There are concrete reasons for believing that experience counts and that more of it is coming your way at any time now. Look out for some unusual advantages and grab them with both hands. The sky is the limit and you cannot afford to ignore events that will broaden your horizons at the moment.

30 SUNDAY
Moon Age Day 14   Moon Sign Aries

General trends remain good and it is really only the lunar low that appears to be holding you back. Let others make some of the running and be content with a moderate pace of events. You won't want to make many important decisions, even though in some ways this period of the month seems to be spurring you on.

October
2012

1 MONDAY
Moon Age Day 15   Moon Sign Aries

There isn't a great deal in the way of assistance today and so you might feel you are going it alone. Try to remember that part of what is happening is related to your emotional state, which in turn responds to the lunar low. Slow and steady wins the race, even if this particular lap is not too eventful.

2 TUESDAY
Moon Age Day 16   Moon Sign Taurus

People are fun to be with and there are very few individuals who try to throw a spanner in the works of any of your ideas. More than one planet is now well placed to give you the edge, which you can work to your advantage. Focus on the domestic scene, which should now provide most of the pleasure you need in your life.

3 WEDNESDAY
Moon Age Day 17   Moon Sign Taurus

Although you may be fairly wrapped up in yourself today, you should still take time out to see the way the world looks from the perspective of another person. Once you do so, the very experience brings you out into the open and forces you to be more sociable again. A solitary Libran is not a happy individual as a rule.

4 THURSDAY
Moon Age Day 18   Moon Sign Taurus

Make your feelings known to people who might think they have upset you in some way and offer them reassurance. This is a time when you tend to retreat, temporarily, from the world. It won't be a phase that stays around long and you are not likely to be sulking about anything. You simply have a need to think things through.

5 FRIDAY
Moon Age Day 19   Moon Sign Gemini

For the moment, living in the middle of a competitive world doesn't seem so attractive, but bear in mind this situation will change within a day. Keep your options open, so that even if you are not actually achieving very much, your thought processes are in operation. Take the time to relax.

6 SATURDAY
Moon Age Day 20   Moon Sign Gemini

You have plenty of get up and go right now, so tackle everything with the same desire to succeed. People from the past may surface again, and may bring with them some news you have been longing to hear for a while. You should enjoy more than a small element of luck in most of your endeavours at present.

7 SUNDAY
Moon Age Day 21   Moon Sign Cancer

It appears that in debates or discussions you may be up against people with strong egos at the moment. However, there is more than one way to skin a cat. If you remain absolutely charming and don't rise to the bait, you will get your own way by default. The sign of Libra can be extremely cunning on occasions.

8 MONDAY
Moon Age Day 22   Moon Sign Cancer

Perhaps you need to look at certain matters with more care today and it would help to keep quiet about them until you have. There are gains to be made, though you will have to look hard to find them. If anything, you are being slightly less consistent today, a good indication that you are not firing on all cylinders.

9 TUESDAY
Moon Age Day 23   Moon Sign Cancer

Making real progress in your work won't be too easy but it is far from certain you will actually care very much about this fact – at least for the next few days. Life can still prove very fulfilling at the moment, mainly as a result of the emotional support coming to you from the direction of loved ones.

10 WEDNESDAY *Moon Age Day 24 Moon Sign Leo*

Probably the best advice that can be offered to Libra today is to ensure that you get one task out of the way before you start on another. There is a danger of overlap and confusion that you could so easily avoid. There ought to be a good deal of happiness about in a family and friendship sense.

11 THURSDAY *Moon Age Day 25 Moon Sign Leo*

You should now find it easier to whisper those intimate little words that can make all the difference in the relationship stakes. Don't be too quick to jump to conclusions in work-related matters. All joint financial matters are especially well starred at present, likewise partnerships with a monetary aspect.

12 FRIDAY *Moon Age Day 26 Moon Sign Virgo*

Socially speaking, this is a good time to meet new people and you may well get rid of some of your associations from the past. Libra is all about change and diversity at present. There are certain signposts to success around now, even if you have to keep your eyes wide open in order to recognise them.

13 SATURDAY *Moon Age Day 27 Moon Sign Virgo*

Although you won't be feeling absolutely positive about everything, you can fool others and even yourself in the end. Improved communication is likely to be the best gift of the weekend. Don't be tardy when it comes to expressing an opinion, even when you know there are people around who will not agree with you.

14 SUNDAY *Moon Age Day 28 Moon Sign Libra*

Hooray! Planetary benefits come your way from a number of different directions whilst the lunar high is present. You can afford to back your hunches and might find yourself sought out by someone you think of as being extremely special. Whatever the weather, you could benefit from spending some time out of doors.

15 MONDAY   *Moon Age Day 0   Moon Sign Libra*

There are some particularly interesting people around during the lunar high, one or two of whom have had their eyes on you for a while. Affection could come from some very surprising directions. Plans should be turning out more or less as you would expect, leaving you with hours on your hands that can be simply used for having fun.

16 TUESDAY   *Moon Age Day 1   Moon Sign Libra*

It is important not to react too strongly today so keep your cool. It is possible for you to score some singular successes, simply by refusing to rise to any bait that is presently offered. You could find the opinions of others to be either irrelevant of even downright annoying now. Patience is a virtue that Libra fortunately possesses.

17 WEDNESDAY   *Moon Age Day 2   Moon Sign Scorpio*

You can probably expect good news somewhere in the family, maybe associated with a new arrival. Concern for your partner may be quite understandable but is probably without real cause. You will now enjoy keeping a high profile, whether at work or out there in the social world.

18 THURSDAY   *Moon Age Day 3   Moon Sign Scorpio*

Travel is definitely recommended both now and over the following three or four days. In sporting activities, you could be doing rather better than you had expected, partly because you are so very competitive right now. A warm and wonderful sort of evening is yours for the taking – don't stay home alone.

19 FRIDAY   *Moon Age Day 4   Moon Sign Sagittarius*

Someone you haven't seen for ages could well turn up later today. Love and romantic developments show progress, as do all associations with the countryside and short journeys. Meanwhile, you need to keep an open mind about the behaviour of a friend, which might be giving cause for concern.

20 SATURDAY   *Moon Age Day 5   Moon Sign Sagittarius*

You are unlikely to be able to get on side with specific individuals, no matter how hard you try. It might be better to concentrate on issues and people you can change. Whilst it is clear that you enjoy communicating and getting your message across, this is more difficult than has been the case during the last couple of weeks.

21 SUNDAY   *Moon Age Day 6   Moon Sign Capricorn*

Unfinished tasks need sorting out today, before you clear the decks for a new task or direction that is waiting in the wings. Putting the finishing touches to anything can be hard for Libra, which frequently has its sights on the next hurdle. However, at this point in time you are going to discover that it is essential.

22 MONDAY   *Moon Age Day 7   Moon Sign Capricorn*

New regimes are at hand, one or two of which ought to make you feel a good deal fitter and better able to cope with pressure. Don't be too quick to judge others, especially regarding personal matters. With more wit and application, your way forward appears to have better signposts than has been the case for a few days.

23 TUESDAY   *Moon Age Day 8   Moon Sign Aquarius*

Freedom of expression is paramount and you are likely to want to let everyone know exactly how you feel. Fortunately you also have astrological trends around at the moment that point to diplomacy and tact so you should be able to make sure you do so without offending anyone.

24 WEDNESDAY   *Moon Age Day 9   Moon Sign Aquarius*

It is important that you get some time to yourself today so that you can do things that please only you. Apart from that, try to focus on minor obligations but don't get carried away with them. All in all, it's the bigger picture that counts and so you should be casting at least part of your mind far into the future.

25 THURSDAY   *Moon Age Day 10   Moon Sign Pisces*

All aspects to do with romance have a great deal going for them this week and the romantic qualities of your nature are almost certain to show around now. This process is a two-way street, so you should not be in the least surprised to find that you are number one on someone else's list.

26 FRIDAY   *Moon Age Day 11   Moon Sign Pisces*

If you find you are having problems regarding commitments or plans, you are likely to find that they are of your own making. Try to take a fairly offhand attitude and simply let life flow where it wants to go. There seems little reason why today should not prove to be entirely different from yesterday.

27 SATURDAY   *Moon Age Day 12   Moon Sign Aries*

It might be sensible to allow others to make the decisions for the moment. The lunar low this month has the effect of making you want to shy away from decisions, which is really unusual for Libra. These trends only last a very short time but don't be surprised if you only want to put your feet up and relax.

28 SUNDAY   *Moon Age Day 13   Moon Sign Aries*

There are practical setbacks today and these can lead to long delays when it comes to doing things you have planned. All you can do is to show a high degree of patience because shouting or stamping your feet simply won't help. In your friendships with others, you have the opportunity to show yourself to be very loyal.

29 MONDAY   *Moon Age Day 14   Moon Sign Aries*

Things gradually improve. Expect to be on a winning streak as far as your work is concerned and don't miss out on any opportunity to get ahead. Colleagues should prove to be very supportive and it appears that the right sort of people are keeping a careful eye on you at the moment. You should feel confident in your own ability to make things happen.

30 TUESDAY · Moon Age Day 15 · Moon Sign Taurus

This is going to be a busy time and it is likely that you will be skipping from one task to the next. Even so, you ought to find this a generally happy and productive day. Personal relationships should be on the up, even if you find that you don't have the time to explore them during the first half of today.

31 WEDNESDAY · Moon Age Day 16 · Moon Sign Taurus

A brief period of high activity is doubtless followed by a more relaxing and enjoyable phase. Some Librans would enjoy a visit to the shops or maybe a trip to the cinema. You have to put a certain matter to bed today before you can begin to enjoy the positive trends that surround you at the moment.

November 2012

1 THURSDAY
Moon Age Day 17   Moon Sign Gemini

Constant communication is very important indeed at present and ensures that everyone is pulling in the same direction. Some rules and regulations could seem entirely pointless. Don't be afraid to make instant decisions in current endeavours and be sure to let those around you know what you are doing.

2 FRIDAY
Moon Age Day 18   Moon Sign Gemini

It would be best to take plenty of time to make up your mind about anything at the moment, so any instant decision-making for Libra is out of the window. Personal plans are subject to change and you need to show a very flexible and even an off-hand approach if you want to seem cool in the eyes of others.

3 SATURDAY
Moon Age Day 19   Moon Sign Gemini

Now you are revealing your hidden assertive side, even if this isn't entirely appropriate. There probably isn't very much time for rest and relaxation but you won't care too much. This is a day of high activity and for some it might be a contrast to everything that has been happening over the last few days.

4 SUNDAY
Moon Age Day 20   Moon Sign Cancer

Have patience, if necessary, at the moment, together with an understanding that things will come out right in the end. Loved ones could prove somewhat difficult to understand or even to talk to. Your expectations of life won't be totally fulfilled today and there are times when you will have to settle for what you see as second best.

5 MONDAY   *Moon Age Day 21   Moon Sign Cancer*

It seems as though expectations are best kept to a minimum today – that way you can't end up too disappointed. Some small failures can be anticipated and if you deal with them as and when they arise, they can even be turned to your advantage. People you don't see too often could figure in your social life.

6 TUESDAY   *Moon Age Day 22   Moon Sign Leo*

Although it seems as though everyone wants to give you advice at this time, in the end it's your own opinions that count. Watch out for financial fluctuations but don't make too much fuss about them right now. You are very astute at present and would not be likely to falter over important decisions.

7 WEDNESDAY   ☿   *Moon Age Day 23   Moon Sign Leo*

People from the past resurface in your life at any time now. Emotional matters are likely to be occupying you fully today. That isn't so unusual, bearing in mind present planetary trends, but such considerations could get in the way of more practical matters that also demand your attention.

8 THURSDAY   ☿   *Moon Age Day 24   Moon Sign Leo*

Out there in the big world there are all sorts of offers and you are in just the right frame of mind to say yes to at least some of them. There are likely to be some very interesting people around at present. Today marks a period during which you should find something new and interesting to occupy your time.

9 FRIDAY   ☿   *Moon Age Day 25   Moon Sign Virgo*

Friends and relatives alike are happy to have you around, so stand by to be the life and soul of any party that attracts your attention today. Popularity is assured and that makes you very happy. It isn't at all hard for you to do several different jobs at the same time, and all with a certain panache that impresses others.

10 SATURDAY ☿ *Moon Age Day 26   Moon Sign Virgo*

Ahead of the lunar high, look out for a fairly nostalgic phase that is coming your way any time now. Although there are warm and comforting aspects to your past, it is the future that really matters. Don't get hung up on things that are long gone – that's not the way Libra makes the best impression on life. Keep planning ahead.

11 SUNDAY ☿ *Moon Age Day 27   Moon Sign Libra*

This period ought to coincide with a new burst of energy and allows you to look at things afresh. Romance is probably your chief resort at the moment and unattached Librans should now be looking around for new love. There can be something deeply sensual about today and you may revel in the general popularity you enjoy.

12 MONDAY ☿ *Moon Age Day 28   Moon Sign Libra*

The ability to attract the good things in life is likely to be extremely strong today, so don't be too shy to get out there and ask for what you need. Personally speaking, you have plenty going for you and can attract all sorts of attention, some of which you weren't even looking for. Remember to be considerate of those around you.

13 TUESDAY ☿ *Moon Age Day 0   Moon Sign Scorpio*

It would be a good day to convince your partner that the time is right to ring the changes at home. There are fulfilling social encounters to be had and it is important to realise at the moment that life is about far more than simply working hard. It is the diversions that really count and you are sure to be attracted by anything old or unusual.

14 WEDNESDAY ☿ *Moon Age Day 1   Moon Sign Scorpio*

The position of the Moon gives a positive aspect to romance today, so keep opportunities in your radar. You might find yourself running out of steam rather easily now that trends are flagging a little, so concentrate on things that really interest you. That way you will be so captivated you won't notice the slight restrictions around.

15 THURSDAY ☿ *Moon Age Day 2   Moon Sign Sagittarius*

As far as relationships are concerned, it is possible you will find something you thought was missing. It could be as simple as the reactions you are getting from someone else, or perhaps a promise that is made today. This is a good time to look for improvements all round at work, not to mention in your personal life right now.

16 FRIDAY ☿ *Moon Age Day 3   Moon Sign Sagittarius*

Although you can't have everything you want today, if you are selective and sensible, much can come your way. Just tone down your manner a notch or two and take time to listen to what others are saying. You could be rather too assertive for your own good and need to curb your enthusiasm somewhat.

17 SATURDAY ☿ *Moon Age Day 4   Moon Sign Capricorn*

Co-operation is clearly one of the keys to success and you will be able to gain attention in group situations. Mostly you find yourself taking the lead and others will follow when exposed to your enthusiasm and magnetic personality. Happy influences abound, pushed along by the position of Mercury in your solar chart.

18 SUNDAY ☿ *Moon Age Day 5   Moon Sign Capricorn*

The positive planetary trends highlight your ability to be self-assured, certain of your ground and extremely loving, so you should use these advantages to make this a memorable day. Your general level of good luck also looks fine but it might not be wise to chance your arm too much. Financially speaking, you may not have to.

19 MONDAY ☿ *Moon Age Day 6   Moon Sign Aquarius*

Romance is possible today. If you look in the right place, you could discover an admirer you didn't know you had, which could be very rewarding. If the day turns out to be busy, make sure you find the time to say the simple things, like I love you. There will be numerous challenges but plenty of potential.

20 TUESDAY ☿ *Moon Age Day 7   Moon Sign Aquarius*

Routines might actually help you today. Much of the time, you are likely to be more interested in getting on well with others rather than making sure jobs are done properly. This isn't entirely unusual for you because your zodiac sign is so friendly but you will have to concentrate on the job at hand for at least part of the time.

21 WEDNESDAY ☿ *Moon Age Day 8   Moon Sign Pisces*

You need to be relaxed today and to spend hours doing more or less whatever suits you at the time. Knowing Libra, this could be almost anything. You can make satisfactory progress in most areas of your life but may actively choose to stay away from work-based situations and considerations if this is at all possible.

22 THURSDAY ☿ *Moon Age Day 9   Moon Sign Pisces*

Making decisions on what is and what is not important is never too difficult for you but you will have to show a great deal of tact because you might find you need to go against the advice of someone you like. Don't believe everything you hear today because a certain percentage of it is not going to be true.

23 FRIDAY ☿ *Moon Age Day 10   Moon Sign Pisces*

The cultured side of Libra is starting to show quite clearly now. You need to concentrate more on financial developments at the moment if you are going to get ahead as much as you would wish. However, this doesn't mean ignoring more personal aspects of life because these too can offer benefits.

24 SATURDAY ☿ *Moon Age Day 11   Moon Sign Aries*

Circumstances hold you back and with the lunar low around it will be really difficult to make the sort of progress you might wish. You can sidestep some of the problems caused by this planetary position by simply allowing others to take some of the strain and encouraging them to make decisions on your behalf.

25 SUNDAY ☿ *Moon Age Day 12   Moon Sign Aries*

Rather than rushing at situations or working against immovable problems, simply wait a day or two. In the meantime, you should let yourself in for a little luxury. Sit back and let others take the strain. Since the lunar low is bound to slow things down somewhat, the best way to get ahead is not to try too hard.

26 MONDAY ☿ *Moon Age Day 13   Moon Sign Taurus*

The days are gradually becoming more stimulating for you and allowing you to show more of that Libran personality to almost anyone you meet. Popularity is high around this time. You need to do your own thing today, that's quite clear, but you have to take the needs of your loved ones on board too.

27 TUESDAY ☿ *Moon Age Day 14   Moon Sign Taurus*

There are a few situations coming along during which it would be good to keep your opinions to yourself. Avoid disputes that are not of your making and don't allow yourself to be put into the position of having to make decisions for other people because there is a danger you will take the blame if things go wrong.

28 WEDNESDAY *Moon Age Day 15   Moon Sign Taurus*

Friendship is extremely important at the moment and there isn't much doubt that you will have the opportunity to show that you cherish pals you have known for years. Confidence grows significantly when you are doing jobs you really understand. This is likely to be a very inspiring day and one that offers you new incentives on a number of different levels.

29 THURSDAY *Moon Age Day 16   Moon Sign Gemini*

There are some very entertaining and interesting people around at this time and they offer significant diversions for this part of the week. However, some Librans will be actively seeking a quieter spell now. Although there might be less fun than you had expected coming from some relationships, the shortfall can be made up by others.

30 FRIDAY
Moon Age Day 17   Moon Sign Gemini

Restlessness is something Librans need to be careful about, particularly at the moment. Give yourself a pat on the back for a success you are scoring at home but don't think the effort stops here. There is further still to go. All in all, you might feel frustrated by the tendency of others to try to hold you back.

December

2012

1 SATURDAY
Moon Age Day 18   Moon Sign Cancer

Getting those close to you to do what is expected of them won't be easy just now but is necessary to your own peace of mind. Try not to push yourself too hard, particularly since there appears to be no special reason for doing so. This is likely to be a day of busy demands and keenly felt responsibilities.

2 SUNDAY
Moon Age Day 19   Moon Sign Cancer

Now comes a time when you should be thinking specifically about romance and the social side of life. This also might now be the first time you have realised that Christmas is just around the corner. Put all thoughts of work behind you, if you can, and take time out to do something that appeals to you.

3 MONDAY
Moon Age Day 20   Moon Sign Cancer

You can easily use present trends to get ahead, though you probably need to lighten up somewhat. Your general manner is less tactful than might be expected for Libra as a rule and you need to exercise a good deal of patience when dealing with people who are naturally inclined to get on your nerves.

4 TUESDAY
Moon Age Day 21   Moon Sign Leo

Although not everyone you meet at present is equally reliable, you ought to find it fairly easy to sort out who you can trust. Turn up your intuition and listen carefully to what it is telling you. This is a day on which it would be wise to follow your instincts, which are unlikely to let you down.

5 WEDNESDAY   *Moon Age Day 22   Moon Sign Leo*

What really sets today apart is the way you should be using your typical Libran nature to bring out the best in others. You have plenty to keep you busy, both inside the family and further afield. This is unlikely to be a totally stay-at-home sort of day for many of you so you should be out there looking to activate the potential excitement.

6 THURSDAY   *Moon Age Day 23   Moon Sign Virgo*

When it comes to personal matters, no matter what other people tell you, it is important to make up your own mind in the end. Dealings with those who are in a position of authority can be important and you need to be willing to cultivate their assistance and advice. Make sure you listen before making up your mind.

7 FRIDAY   *Moon Age Day 24   Moon Sign Virgo*

If the social whirl has begun already, you need to be sure that you are getting enough rest. Perhaps you could try only going out six nights a week, leaving at least one on which you can rest! You have the potential to be on top form at work today, which in turn could lead to a few successes you haven't really been expecting.

8 SATURDAY   *Moon Age Day 25   Moon Sign Libra*

The lunar high finds you quite organised, though still inclined to go it alone more than would often be the case. Nevertheless, you do show a very positive face to the world at just about every level of your life. This is the best time during this month for getting the maximum amount done in the shortest time possible.

9 SUNDAY   *Moon Age Day 26   Moon Sign Libra*

Enjoying personal freedom is not at all difficult. It is time to capitalise on a new opportunity and to make the most of small financial gains that should be coming your way around now. If you don't do something novel or different at the moment, you might end up regretting this in time.

10 MONDAY   *Moon Age Day 27   Moon Sign Scorpio*

This may prove to be the best part of the month for telling someone how very special they are and for enjoying a busy time socially. You will need to focus some of your attention on career and related matters, though probably not for very long, and you may need to project your thoughts towards things happening in a few days.

11 TUESDAY   *Moon Age Day 28   Moon Sign Scorpio*

You can do with all the support that is available at this busy time and you should not be too worried about delegating some of the responsibility. As may have been the case earlier this month, you need to be aware that confidence tricksters are about. Loved ones can be in the market to offer great favours today so ask for what you need.

12 WEDNESDAY   *Moon Age Day 0   Moon Sign Sagittarius*

Although some of the things you are dealing with today may not seem to be important, in reality you should be receptive to learning a great deal. Relatives should be especially warm and involve you in matters that can prove very satisfying. You cannot afford to miss out on socialising or to avoid the cut and thrust of a busy day.

13 THURSDAY   *Moon Age Day 1   Moon Sign Sagittarius*

You are inclined to be rather energetic today and may not spend too much time sitting around and thinking. Periods of high activity are not at all unusual for Libra but you will be busy at the moment, even by your own standards. This is a good time for introducing variety into your leisure and pleasure activities.

14 FRIDAY   *Moon Age Day 2   Moon Sign Capricorn*

Probably the best areas to spend your time on today are with regard to personal relationships and the way you see friendships developing. A small injection of unexpected cash could now be on the cards. Things begin to go your way in a more concrete sense and you ought to have little trouble with life today.

15 SATURDAY   *Moon Age Day 3   Moon Sign Capricorn*

A high social profile on your part is the most satisfying way forward around now, although you should also find it relatively simple to put things together on the material plane. Few people are causing you too much concern and it is more than possible that a new relationship is about to start.

16 SUNDAY   *Moon Age Day 4   Moon Sign Aquarius*

Regardless of the season or the weather, this would be an ideal day to make a trip designed purely for pleasure, rather than for business. Love-life encounters have a fulfilling quality about them now, leading you to bring romantic issues to the forefront and to enjoy what they are offering.

17 MONDAY   *Moon Age Day 5   Moon Sign Aquarius*

There ought to be informative and pleasant Christmas-based social encounters in the offing today. Don't let matters slide where your best-laid plans are concerned. It is important to concentrate and, once again, to look at situations one at a time. The broad overview, which is typical of your nature, won't work so well today.

18 TUESDAY   *Moon Age Day 6   Moon Sign Aquarius*

Perhaps someone in the family is seeing things your way to a greater extent, or it could just be that you have reached a stage during which you think you know best. You feel more able to express yourself today, most probably because you are released from a few constraints that have been surrounding you in the recent past.

19 WEDNESDAY   *Moon Age Day 7   Moon Sign Pisces*

Some planetary aspects harden, meaning this is a time when you are likely to speak your mind, perhaps a little too bluntly. Much more matter-of-fact than usual, you may not seem quite so charming, though there are people who will find it easier to get along with you all the same. Get on with practical matters, positively aspected by the Sun.

20 THURSDAY · *Moon Age Day 8 · Moon Sign Pisces*

You should be good at multi-tasking today, which in turn should give you the chance of a very happy and stress-free evening. Your work life could prove to be an area of potential pressure, which is all the more reason for you to do almost anything to let your hair down when the professional responsibilities are out of the way.

21 FRIDAY · *Moon Age Day 9 · Moon Sign Aries*

The lunar low can prove to be a disruptive influence today, possibly leading you to doubt your own abilities and certainly bringing a quieter day than you had probably been expecting. What you can do now is to plan for Christmas, which is much closer than you have realised.

22 SATURDAY · *Moon Age Day 10 · Moon Sign Aries*

Look out for repeated delays and setbacks, some of which cannot be avoided no matter how hard you try. In fact, it isn't really worth trying at all. To do so represents the equivalent of trying to push water up hill. Accept what life is offering with a smile and simply wait for more advantageous times.

23 SUNDAY · *Moon Age Day 11 · Moon Sign Taurus*

Although you might discuss present trends and happenings with people you trust, it will still be you who makes up your own mind in the end. Within your discussions lies a necessary degree of reassurance. There are probably some very big decisions to be made today, and you could be quite reticent about addressing them alone.

24 MONDAY · *Moon Age Day 12 · Moon Sign Taurus*

Christmas Eve is definitely a day for getting out and about and for making new contacts. Some of these are going to be of tremendous importance later on. Little by little, changes that you are making to your life are beginning to have a bearing on your success. At least some time today should be spent dealing with younger relatives.

25 TUESDAY   *Moon Age Day 13   Moon Sign Taurus*

It is the interesting information offered to you by Christmas Day that keeps you both entertained and happy. Libra is now a very definite party animal and you are clearly making up for a slightly quieter interval that may have come before Christmas itself. The message of the season isn't lost on you when it comes to people who are less well off than you are.

26 WEDNESDAY   *Moon Age Day 14   Moon Sign Gemini*

With communication very much to the fore, you may spend Boxing Day talking to others – whether personally or by phone, text or email doesn't matter much. A day of much gadding about is forecast, though that won't prevent you from looking deeply into specific matters that are of personal interest to you right now.

27 THURSDAY   *Moon Age Day 15   Moon Sign Gemini*

You may find that there is a great deal of coming and going again today, so much so that you might find it difficult to concentrate on anything at all. Maybe that's no bad thing. Specifics are not what your life is about right now so accept that you need to be looking at the general picture rather than the detail.

28 FRIDAY   *Moon Age Day 16   Moon Sign Cancer*

Exactly the right words to please your lover seem to be eluding you for the moment, though this may not be your fault at all. Entertaining people at home is the best way to enjoy your social life at the moment.

29 SATURDAY   *Moon Age Day 17   Moon Sign Cancer*

Don't give in to the tendency to hold back in any situation simply because you doubt the reaction of those around you. You have things to say, and if you do, you'll find people willing to listen.

30 SUNDAY   *Moon Age Day 18   Moon Sign Cancer*

It isn't like Libra to take big risks, but there are some calculated risks around at present that you should consider. Money matters should be better and you are keeping the necessities of the future well in view.

31 MONDAY   *Moon Age Day 19   Moon Sign Leo*

Things should be looking good and you probably won't bother with New Year resolutions. For the moment you make life up as you go along and that's fine. This could be a day of considerable boons on a material level. You have more than your fair share of good luck.

30 SUNDAY

31 MONDAY

RISING SIGNS FOR LIBRA

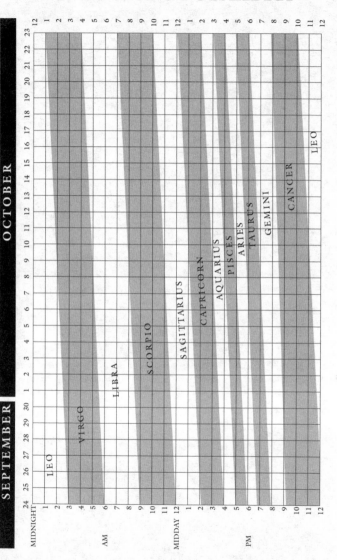

THE ZODIAC, PLANETS AND CORRESPONDENCES

The Earth revolves around the Sun once every calendar year, so when viewed from Earth the Sun appears in a different part of the sky as the year progresses. In astrology, these parts of the sky are divided into the signs of the zodiac and this means that the signs are organised in a circle. The circle begins with Aries and ends with Pisces.

Taking the zodiac sign as a starting point, astrologers then work with all the positions of planets, stars and many other factors to calculate horoscopes and birth charts and tell us what the stars have in store for us.

The table below shows the planets and Elements for each of the signs of the zodiac. Each sign belongs to one of the four Elements: Fire, Air, Earth or Water. Fire signs are creative and enthusiastic; Air signs are mentally active and thoughtful; Earth signs are constructive and practical; Water signs are emotional and have strong feelings.

It also shows the metals and gemstones associated with, or corresponding with, each sign. The correspondence is made when a metal or stone possesses properties that are held in common with a particular sign of the zodiac.

Finally, the table shows the opposite of each star sign – this is the opposite sign in the astrological circle.

Placed	Sign	Symbol	Element	Planet	Metal	Stone	Opposite
1	Aries	Ram	Fire	Mars	Iron	Bloodstone	Libra
2	Taurus	Bull	Earth	Venus	Copper	Sapphire	Scorpio
3	Gemini	Twins	Air	Mercury	Mercury	Tiger's Eye	Sagittarius
4	Cancer	Crab	Water	Moon	Silver	Pearl	Capricorn
5	Leo	Lion	Fire	Sun	Gold	Ruby	Aquarius
6	Virgo	Maiden	Earth	Mercury	Mercury	Sardonyx	Pisces
7	Libra	Scales	Air	Venus	Copper	Sapphire	Aries
8	Scorpio	Scorpion	Water	Pluto	Plutonium	Jasper	Taurus
9	Sagittarius	Archer	Fire	Jupiter	Tin	Topaz	Gemini
10	Capricorn	Goat	Earth	Saturn	Lead	Black Onyx	Cancer
11	Aquarius	Waterbearer	Air	Uranus	Uranium	Amethyst	Leo
12	Pisces	Fishes	Water	Neptune	Tin	Moonstone	Virgo